The MIT Press Essential Knowledge Series

A complete list of books in this series can be found online at
https://mitpress.mit.edu/books/series/mit-press-essential-knowledge-series.

PRAGMATISM

JOHN R. SHOOK

The MIT Press | Cambridge, Massachusetts | London, England

The MIT Press would like to thank the anonymous peer reviewers who provided comments on drafts of this book. The generous work of academic experts is essential for establishing the authority and quality of our publications. We acknowledge with gratitude the contributions of these otherwise uncredited readers.

This book was set in Chaparral Pro by New Best-set Typesetters Ltd. Printed and bound in the United States of America.

Library of Congress Cataloging-in-Publication Data

Names: Shook, John R., author.
Title: Pragmatism / John R. Shook.
Description: Cambridge, Massachusetts : The MIT Press, 2023 | Series: MIT Press essential knowledge series | Includes bibliographical references and index.
Identifiers: LCCN 2021057612 | ISBN 9780262544610 (paperback)
Subjects: LCSH: Pragmatism.
Classification: LCC B8332 .S48 2023 | DDC 144/.3—dc23/eng/20211202
LC record available at https://lccn.loc.gov/2021057612

10 9 8 7 6 5 4 3 2 1

CONTENTS

SERIES FOREWORD

The MIT Press Essential Knowledge series offers accessible, concise, beautifully produced pocket-size books on topics of current interest. Written by leading thinkers, the books in this series deliver expert overviews of subjects that range from the cultural and the historical to the scientific and the technical.

In today's era of instant information gratification, we have ready access to opinions, rationalizations, and superficial descriptions. Much harder to come by is the foundational knowledge that informs a principled understanding of the world. Essential Knowledge books fill that need. Synthesizing specialized subject matter for nonspecialists and engaging critical topics through fundamentals, each of these compact volumes offers readers a point of access to complex ideas.

PREFACE

Any book about an intellectual movement, limited to 50,000 words and denied a subtitle, couldn't cover everything implied by its title. A humble preface leading with the fitting subtitle can apologize for what was not written, as well as what was. Much about pragmatism is regrettably absent. To speak in its defense, this book is neither a survey nor a summary. When did pragmatism reach a finality, that it might be stated summarily?

To keep pragmatism useful, its key philosophical proposals can be inventoried in preparation for further application. Chapters explain how pragmatism thinks about what is real, what can be known, and what minds are doing. This book seeks a wider audience than just philosophers, since pragmatism was designed for impacts well beyond philosophy. Every academic discipline has been influenced by pragmatism, and many rely on its continued relevance. Having this book's lessons in hand while looking into principles of various fields can guide the non-philosopher through philosophical foundations as they come into view.

As for philosophers, dense and direct chapters may seem more polemical than practical. No apology seems necessary there. Clarity through contrast with rival positions has philosophical merit. Charity has merit too.

Pragmatism has earned its reputation as a conciliator among "isms" to negotiate bridgings and blendings.

All the same, pragmatism insists on revising or replacing rigid tenets that have dominated Western thought. Intellectual confrontations, especially when civilizations reach historical junctures, are unavoidable. At such times, disciplinary cohesiveness is paramount, and supportive alliances among philosophies have their place. Putting on record what pragmatism distinctively offers could not be out of place either.

Far too many academic debts among pragmatist colleagues have accumulated to be listed here. Let a dedication stand: To the memory of Joseph Margolis (1924–2021), whose death dimmed, but could not extinguish, the leading light of Columbia pragmatic naturalism.

Alexandria, Virginia
Summer 2022

PRAGMATISM

An Old Name for Newly Confirmed Ideas

"Pragmatism" names an intellectual movement with American origins, but its ideas travel everywhere. Rarely does a philosophy join the great systems of thought while securing a place in the popular imagination. Stoicism illustrates that combination from antiquity, and humanism is the Renaissance contribution, with liberalism, existentialism, and pragmatism serving as modern examples.

While appealing to the modern mind's wide curiosity and appetite for exploration, pragmatist thinking is far older than its apt name. Precursors and partners can be found in Western philosophies, Eastern thought, and Indigenous wisdom traditions.

Perennial systems of thought ponder what it means to be human while speculating about mind's essence, life's nature, and the cosmos's origins. Pragmatism finds our common humanity in the intelligent pursuit of earthly opportunities and worthy aspirations.

No honest appreciation of what we accomplish as a species, from art and ritual to technology and science, has yet disagreed. Disparaging our practical intelligence and doubting human ideals is the occupation of philosophies preferring unearthly pursuits and otherworldly ends. Pointedly non-dualistic and humanistic, pragmatists offer integrations of mentality and biological vitality within a dynamic cosmology. Life is not only worth living, it is worth living *better*.

Pragmatism, a System

This book explains core views of pragmatism about reality, truth, knowledge, science, mind, society, and culture. Along the way, contrasts are drawn with tenets of rival worldviews. It culminates with pragmatism's theories of social psychology, ecological mentality, and philosophical anthropology. There we must halt. However, this groundwork can guide the reader's further explorations of pragmatist approaches to normative areas such as aesthetics, ethics, politics, law, technology, education, and religion.

Pragmatism's primary exponents receive the most attention: Charles Sanders Peirce (1839–1914), William James (1842–1910), John Dewey (1859–1952), and George Herbert Mead (1863–1931). It would be unpragmatic to expect good pragmatism only from its original thinkers. Contemporary pragmatism is featured in many chapters. Key principles from founders remain consistent with, and confirmed by, subsequent scientific and scholarly advances.

Generations after the founders down to the present have reinvigorated pragmatism with refined versions. Some have been called "neo-pragmatism" or "new pragmatism." Just a few years after Peirce's death in 1914, Charles Morris, who was Mead's colleague at the University of Chicago, announced his "Neo-Pragmatism" with due genuflection towards James and Dewey as well as Peirce. There have been "new" pragmatisms ever since, in spirit if not in name.[1]

Many thinkers have effectively rediscovered pragmatism, while unacquainted with its heritage. Some disavow "pragmatism" due to half-remembered distortions of its founders kept in circulation by opposed philosophies. Pragmatism carries on as a perennial philosophy based on principles, not personalities. That openness is characteristic of pragmatism. There is no esoteric discourse, obscure doctrine, or devout discipleship. Whenever philosophical thought appreciates life's historical contingencies and intelligence's productive capacities, it becomes more like pragmatism in practice.

Pragmatism is unlike other "-isms" labelling specific theses or ideologies, such as "socialism" and "capitalism" in economics, or "conservativism" in politics. The "ism" of pragmatism denotes a systemic worldview: cohesive principles and tenets for philosophy's primary domains. Pragmatist views on reality, truth, knowledge, and cognition (topics for metaphysics, logic, epistemology, and philosophy of mind) are coordinated with its approaches to morality, justice, beauty, and value generally (treated in ethics, politics, aesthetics, and axiology).

Pragmatism can therefore advise and critique theories about humanity, language, culture, the arts, social organization, religion, government, law, education, mathematics, science, technology, and any of life's endeavors. Unlike most philosophical schools of thought, pragmatism is applicable in every humanistic and academic field, and many disciplinary advances have contributed to pragmatism in return. Limited space prevents any survey of pragmatic theories in aesthetics, ethics, politics, culture studies, philosophy of science and technology, and philosophy of religion, although the last chapters outline principled bases to those contributions.

Pragmatism has a system, it must be reiterated. This book is not yet another exegetical survey of major pragmatists, one by one. Nor shall pragmatism be treated as a cluster of renegade ideas sharing only a family resemblance. Each pragmatist is worthy of close study, without question. Contrasts among them are just as important as agreements. Many books already explore divergences among their distinctive views.[2] Commentaries have attempted to discover two, three, four, or more pragmatisms, and even within a single pragmatist's writings!

If pragmatism could stand for almost anything, its intellectual value would fall to practically nothing. After pragmatism has been reduced to subjectivism or relativism, or linked to hedonism or utilitarianism, or classed as yet another anti-foundationalism or post-modernism, little meaning for pragmatism is left. As this book explains, pragmatism is not divided or directionless. "Pragmatic" sounds contrary to "principled"—but pragmatism offers principled stands about philosophy's main areas and perennial issues. This book explains why there is one philosophical worldview, rightly called pragmatism, and upheld by pragmatists as they enlarge its applicability to life.

Initial chapters of this book explain the foundations to pragmatism. It was never just a theory of mind, knowledge, or truth, although those topics earned pragmatism the most attention, and the most scorn. Only a complete philosophical worldview could suffice to attain the goal of surmounting all previous philosophies and achieving a reconciliation of the humanities with the sciences.

Peirce led the way with the most original system since Baruch Spinoza, Kant, and G. W. F. Hegel, uniting metaphysics, semiotics, and logic to account for the growth of mind within the development of the cosmos. His theories about truth and knowledge assisted James with his own empiricist and pluralistic philosophy. Dewey in turn assembled his own version of empirical naturalism to match his philosophy of culture. Contacts and overlaps with the social and natural sciences are welcomed by such all-encompassing philosophies.

Present-day social and behavioral sciences are reconfirming pragmatist views. Contemporary pragmatism is allied with theories of developmental psychology, the unconscious, reason–emotion–volition integration, neuroplasticity, embodied cognition, and extended mentality. These theories had prototypes in the writings of Classical pragmatists. Combating any philosophy depicting the mind as basically passive, impressionable, intuitive, reflective, representational, or mechanistic, the classical pragmatists sought to understand mentality within its biological and social environs.

Pragmatists refused to bifurcate what is natural apart from what is cultural, lending philosophical support for scientific inquiries into the origins of humanity's distinctive proclivities for art, language, community, and myth. Pragmatism is skeptical towards claims that rationalistic, metaphysical, or theological frameworks are necessary for explaining human creativity, reason, or personhood. In social theory and politics, pragmatism emphasizes historicism, cultural diversity, social justice, and liberal democracy.

Pragmatism would not have joined the great systems of philosophy, and antagonized venerable worldviews, unless it offered novel and penetrating views on fundamental matters about reality and our place in it. Pragmatism is among a handful of movements which prioritizes change and impermanence over form and permanence, deprioritizes necessity and certainty for knowledge and truth, and depicts individuality and sociality as codependently interfused.

Pragmatism is further distinguished by appealing to continuities, contexts, and potentialities to overcome dualities; understanding everything about mind and cognition in evolutionary, developmental, and practical terms; and by studying manifestations of human conduct and life's activity in interrelated and ecological ways.

Pragmatism, in Conception

Harvard psychologist and philosopher William James brought widespread attention to the nascent pragmatist movement with his 1907 book *Pragmatism*, composed from talks given in academic and public lecture halls. Its subtitle was *A New Name for Some Old Ways of Thinking*. Gazing back in time across a plethora of abstraction-ridden rationalisms and scholasticisms, all entranced by otherworldly ends, James embraced the minority opposition focused on worldly matters of actual experience.

His opening dedication page reads as follows: "To the Memory of John Stuart Mill, from whom I first learned the pragmatic openness of mind and whom my fancy likes to picture as our leader were he alive to-day." Mill had died thirty-four years earlier, in 1873, when James was just 31, during an era when empirical science had few philosophical allies. James himself would die just three years after *Pragmatism* as philosophical hostilities towards science were reaching a crescendo. Theologies, idealisms, dualisms, and phenomenologies outbid each other to prove science's incompetence to fully know reality. Positivism and materialism were deemed unphilosophical, while tolerable realisms must pair the objective world with subjective minds knowing it. Empiricism was yet again in a precarious condition.

James boldly called for allies to rally under this new banner of pragmatism. He declared,

> Pragmatism represents a perfectly familiar attitude
> in philosophy, the empiricist attitude, but it
> represents it, as it seems to me, both in a more
> radical and in a less objectionable form than it
> has ever yet assumed. A pragmatist turns his back
> resolutely and once for all upon a lot of inveterate
> habits dear to professional philosophers. He turns
> away from abstraction and insufficiency, from verbal
> solutions, from bad a priori reasons, from fixed

principles, closed systems, and pretended absolutes and origins. He turns towards concreteness and adequacy, towards facts, towards action, and towards power. That means the empiricist temper regnant, and the rationalist temper sincerely given up. It means the open air and possibilities of nature, as against dogma, artificiality and the pretence of finality in truth.[3]

James profited from rebellious alliances, going back to the days of his apprenticeship in philosophy. Mill's empiricism, along with Kant's transcendentalism and Darwinian evolution, was hotly debated by the young Harvard companions forming the Metaphysical Club in Cambridge during the 1870s.

Chauncey Wright had received Darwin's encouragement to address evolution's implications for psychology and mental philosophy. Nicholas St. John Green and Charles Peirce were impressed by Alexander Bain, another British philosopher and psychologist, who declared that belief is "that upon which a man is prepared to act."[4] Peirce went on to conduct psychological experiments at Johns Hopkins University. John Dewey took courses on logic and scientific method from Peirce and learned psychology from G. Stanley Hall, the next Johns Hopkins psychologist, who had been James's student at Harvard. James himself, of course, was well known for psychology as much as philosophy while he was composing *Pragmatism*.

Attention to *experiencing* was paramount for the empiricist agenda. Yet James also depicted pragmatism as a way of thinking about *thinking*: what thinking actually is and what it is for, to understand how thinking goes right. James championed the empirical-minded type of philosopher who constantly contends with rationalism. Pairing a better theory of perceptual learning with an outdated rationalist view of thinking just obscures empiricism's strengths and exposes it to rationalist refutation.

Empiricism's strengths lay in its receptivity to novelty and creativity. When compared to rationalism's fixation on conceptual deduction, empiricism's inductions from phenomena seem fickle and fragmentary. Truth itself was at stake. Shall truth only amount to beliefs already familiar and undeniable? There is no place for genuine discovery within an intellect that is deductively closed. New and unsettling truths are always inconceivable to incurious minds clinging to ideas of the past. All the while, improved knowledge, vast knowledge, lies in the future.

Pragmatism is truly about the future. No truth is too good for testing its worth in that future. James announced, "The true is the name of whatever proves itself to be good in the way of belief, and good, too, for definite, assignable reasons."[5] What makes any truth true is neither its easy conceivability nor its past popularity, but only its ongoing reliability.

> Pragmatism . . . asks its usual question. "Grant an idea or belief to be true," it says, "what concrete difference will its being true make in anyone's actual life? How will the truth be realized? What experiences will be different from those which would obtain if the belief were false? What, in short, is the truth's cash-value in experiential terms?" . . . The truth of an idea is not a stagnant property inherent in it. Truth *happens* to an idea. It *becomes* true, is *made* true by events. Its verity *is* in fact an event, a process: the process namely of its verifying itself, its veri-*fication*. Its validity is the process of its valid-*ation*.[6]

With these incendiary words, the revolution had its declaration of independence from rationalism. The contested territory of reality was not forgotten by either camp in this war of words. Doesn't the way that reality actually is make truths about the world true? A real thing can truly be, today, without waiting for verification tomorrow. Rationalism has its own allies, such as this commonsense realism. Creating truth by human verification sounds like creating the realities to be known.

"The truth of an idea is not a stagnant property inherent in it. Truth happens to an idea. It becomes true, is made true by events."
—William James

Even James's first pragmatist ally, Peirce, scorned that anti-realism: "there are certain mummified pedants who have never waked to the truth that the act of knowing a real object alters it . . . I am one of them."[7] However, like Peirce's dictums about truth, James was not asking for anyone's knowing the truth to create the *object* of knowledge. For the pragmatists, verification creates knowledge, and all they demand is the real object's *participation* in that verification. James was perpetually dismayed by critics who had to complain that this requirement sounds like an unrealistic burden on realities.

This pragmatic demand, for any real thing to matter somewhere, is no less realistic than any rationalism's realism, since verification could not be a threat to anything real. Only unreal things, after all, would fail their verifications. Why shouldn't truth be rooted in the way that things get known as real? Reality should not resist its own realization. Does common sense realism think that just any idea is true, before any verification? Verified knowledge is labeled as "truth" after verification, not before. Before any verification, ideas are just ideas, without anyone possibly knowing if reality backs them up.

A philosophy that allows reality to be just as one thinks would be anti-realism, not pragmatism, as James kept insisting in his subsequent books *The Meaning of Truth* (1909) and *A Pluralistic Universe* (1909). Self-proclaimed defenders of realism were just as insistent that knowing is a mental activity, but mentality must not affect reality just by knowing it. Assigning to mentality the task of creating true realities agrees with idealism. The realists of James's day were trying to put a century of idealism's domination over philosophy to an end. The reign of theology over collegiate education was ending, and the realist camp wanted just one paradigm for professionalized university philosophy. Neither idealism nor pragmatism was deemed compatible with its strict realism.

James was well aware of the high stakes for professional philosophers, but academic philosophy was not his only audience. Changing the whole intellectual world along with the minds of the masses required a masterful stroke. Artful language had to be employed with rhetorical and dialectical skill. The popular imagination can be captured, but radical-sounding words become stale slogans as the fervor fades.

Detractors have no lack of straw-man statements about what pragmatism means. Is truth only what is useful to believe? Do truths multiply with profitable opinions? Must knowledge bend to power? Is reason just desire's servant? Pragmatism stood accused of disintegrating the harmonious cosmos into the playground of willful egos and degrading humanity's proud intellect down to the level of plodding animals.

James was undaunted. After publishing his book *Pragmatism*, James wrote to his brother Henry about pragmatism's impact: "of the definitive triumph of that general way of thinking I can entertain no doubt whatever— I believe it to be something quite like the protestant reformation."[8]

Like religious reformations, philosophical revolutions are never brief and decisive. Over the past hundred years, pragmatism's dramatic rise, prolonged diffusion across the humanities and social sciences, and its recent reinvigoration, fulfills his prediction about the intellectual world needing ample time to debate, digest, and incorporate radical ideas. Philosophy resisted integration the longest, while caricaturing pragmatism as a nest of fallacies. Having purged history, anthropology, sociology, and psychology, rationalisms kept on debating how to dissect reasoning by no one in particular about nothing in particular.

Pragmatism, in Context

Competing movements in English-language philosophy and continental European philosophy could agree on accusing pragmatism of subjectivism, psychologism, relativism, and irrealism. Pragmatism emerged and matured during a period when most every philosophical system had advocates and active schools of thought.

From 1860 to 1940, the variety was bewildering: many varieties of idealism and transcendentalism flourished and jostled with versions of phenomenalism and phenomenology; realisms ranged broadly from dualistic empiricism to scholasticism; and naturalistic options debated positivism, materialism, epiphenomenalism, and scientism. Stoicisms, existentialisms, nihilisms, vitalisms, panpsychisms, spiritualisms, theodicies, and mysticisms were also promoted and pondered.[9]

That profusion of philosophical speculation had dramatically subsided for post-WWII philosophy. Academic philosophy weeded out most of the wildness and narrowed the focus of surviving analytic and phenomenological alternatives. In the process, according to an oft-told tale, pragmatism suffered a long "eclipse" during the second half of the twentieth century.

This myth was itself a myth. Pragmatism was never eclipsed, although it was marginalized within academic philosophy by the 1930s. A handful of pragmatist professors such as Dewey at Columbia, and Mead and Morris at Chicago, had encouraged many students to go into psychology, linguistics, sociology, anthropology, education, economics, law, and political theory. Additional social thinkers such as W. E. B. DuBois, Horace Kallen, Randolph Bourne, Walter Lippmann, Alain LeRoy Locke, C. Wright Mills, and Richard Rorty sustained pragmatism's momentum on addressing social and political issues.[10] That combined infusion of progressivism with pragmatism strongly influenced many disciplines from the 1940s to the 1990s and beyond.

Even in philosophy, departments at Harvard, Chicago, and Columbia remained hospitable to pragmatism, and several of America's prominent philosophers favored pragmatist themes. C. I. Lewis at Harvard taught pragmatism to two generations of students who went on to teach at many top universities. W. V. Quine stayed at Harvard, soon joined by Hilary Putnam, and some of their students have defended pragmatist ideas, such as Donald Davidson. Renegade analytic philosophers, among them Richard Rorty, Daniel Dennett, and Paul Churchland, also ensured that pragmatism remained a potent influence.

Led by this revived pragmatism, philosophy became more receptive to interdisciplinarity with the humanities and social sciences during the 1990s. Even core "analytic" areas such as philosophy of language, epistemology, philosophy of mind, and philosophy of science were impacted. Invigorating encounters with the fields of intellectual history, anthropology, linguistics, behavioral psychology, and cognitive science (just to name a few), brought academic philosophy back into contact with flourishing pragmatist views. As philosophy was figuring out how to be relevant, it was returning to pragmatism.

Within academic philosophy, pragmatism's renaissance has only gained momentum since the 1980s when Putman and Rorty incited fresh debates over the nature of language, knowledge, truth, and the mind–world relationship. Functional psychology, initiated by James and Dewey (who also discovered holistic experience before Gestalt psychology), was revived in a variety of forms, whether labeled as enactive, embodied, extended, or ecological (and so on) to exemplify contextualism and dynamism.

During the 1990s and early 2000s, much of experimental psychology, cognitive science, and neuroscience took pragmatist turns away from lingering dualisms, rationalisms, and representationalisms. Social sciences from psychology to anthropology have been reconfirming the foundations of pragmatism with fresh non-dualistic approaches to cognition and culture. Semiotics, which had largely sprung from pragmatism, is presently supportive of pragmatism's fast-growing movement.

In Europe, pragmatism has been highly regarded by a few phenomenologists (such as Maurice Merleau-Ponty and Alfred Schütz) and some critical theorists (notably Jürgen Habermas), along with discriminating postmodernists (in deconstruction and hermeneutics, for example).[11]

In the humanities, pragmatist revivals did not wait for science's confirmations, plunging ahead with departures from modernism, formalism, and structuralism in order to cultivate respect for history, diversity, and pluralism. Pragmatists have collaborated with religious naturalism and liberal theology, and especially process philosophy and panentheism. Pragmatists are also contributing to political theory, applied ethics, environmental ethics, and philosophy of technology.

Summary

By the 2010s, revolts from mechanistic and reductionist paradigms were gaining momentum, flourishing under unfamiliar labels but recognizably pragmatic nonetheless. Their common pragmatist spirit investigates how thinking and knowing undergo modifications and develop over time through their application, so that growth can characterize *how* we know, along with the growth of *what* we know.

For pragmatism old and new, there is nothing about mentality or rationality entirely aloof from biological development, cultural practice, or intellectual refinement. Experimentally improving ways of knowing is the characteristic work of practiced intelligence, culminating in pedagogical and philosophical reflections on refining the best intellectual methods.

Pragmatism not only thinks but *works*. All aspects of life are actually or potentially responsive to intelligence's attention and reconstruction, including values, norms, and morals. There is nothing about humanity—from the affective and aesthetic to the ethical and political—that is irredeemably irrational or immune from improvement.

PRINCIPLES OF PRAGMATISM

Perennial pragmatism attends to wisdom gathered and preserved about this worldly life. Modern pragmatism incorporates scientific knowledge with that wisdom for lasting philosophical insight. An identification of pragmatism with natural science alone would be unwise. Pragmatism is about culture as much as nature. No divorce between humanistic and scientific outlooks is possible with pragmatism. Science is a thoroughly human endeavor, and nothing human stays inscrutable to science.

New human sciences from 1860 to the early 1900s were inspirational for pragmatism. Biology became evolutionary; neurology mapped brain functionality; psychology revealed thinking's practicality; sociology observed mind's communality; and anthropology explored culture's adaptivity. Pragmatists promptly recognized their overlaps, with each field reinforcing the next. The expectation for each field of knowledge to be organized by distinctive first principles, a widespread supposition since Immanuel Kant, had no place in pragmatism.

Pragmatism, in Theory

Distinguishing natural sciences from human sciences according to their respective methodological principles could ensure that both of their ontologies are equally real. This was an urgent philosophical issue by the mid- to late-1800s.

John Stuart Mill assigned the "moral sciences" in his *A System of Logic* (1843) to the study of mental, social, cultural, and ethical matters in empirically rigorous ways. Separating the Nomothetic (natural) and Idiographic (social) sciences was proposed by Neo-Kantian philosopher Wilhelm Windelband. Wilhelm Dilthey widened this categorization, speaking of the Naturwissenschaften (natural sciences) and the Geisteswissenschaften (human or cultural sciences).[1] Separating ontologies from direct conflict halted materialism's advance. However, philosophy lost interest in tracking where sciences were converging, especially theorizing that violated Kantian strictures about lawful necessity and anti-telic naturality.

The pragmatists rebelled against Kantian dualisms and instead looked to supportive precursors in philosophy and science. Earlier German philosophers, particularly Johann Gottfried von Herder, Friedrich Wilhelm Joseph Schelling, and Johann Wolfgang von Goethe, had argued that nature's ways are hospitable to life's ends. Sciences from physics and chemistry to biology and physiology were postulating a far more dynamic and purposive kind of natural world than Newtonian mechanics could license.[2]

Nature is replete with vitality in fundamental and ineliminable ways, due to molecular polarities and affinities, and chemical receptivities, syntheses, and cyclicities. The rule that only mechanical forces are real in the world, while hints of design and purpose are illusions in the mind, did not comport with most sciences. Everything at and above the molecular level appeared to be busily engaging with select matters around it, acquiring complex patterns that tend towards coordination, harmonization, and perpetuation.

Life cannot just be insensate matter in linear motion. Selectivity and striving are built into the organic world, from the level of organic chemistry all the way up to multicellularity, animality, and large-population sociality. Evolutionary biology showed how the developmental history of any form of life or human way of life is far more explanatory than causal forces. Even relationships between the physical and mental, such as Hermann von Helmholtz's discovery that the perceived intensity of sound or color is proportional to the logarithm of the stimulus intensity, showed how mind is transformative with nature rather than derivative from nature.

Systemic ecological activity occurs at every scale. Ecology, in other words, begins inside cells, not outside in habitats. Goal-seeking activity is no less real than pointless reactivity; life and its pursuits are embedded within nature and are no less natural than atoms.

By the 1880s and '90s, many scientific-minded thinkers realized how Newtonian mechanics must be the artificial mental construct, rather than the empirical observations of organic ends. There was no need to assign different first principles to the natural sciences, life sciences, and human sciences. They all studied the one realm of nature, but at different scopes, scales, and timelines of natural activity.

Strands of this historicism, romanticism, organicism, and voluntarism impacted each of the original pragmatists during their formative stages. Peirce admitted that his system was closest to Schelling's; James's main influences were Wilhelm Wundt (a Schellingian) and Hermann Lotze (a voluntarist); Dewey's early idealism was more Aristotelian and organicist than Hegelian; and Mead was a rapt student of James and Wundt.[3] None of them were materialists, because they respected the sciences for their combined results.

Their pragmatism was uninterested in distinguishing scientific fields according to first principles, especially after sciences began sharing theoretical entities and laboratory results. If chemical affinities account for molecular enchainings, in turn explaining cellular metabolisms that modulate tissue activation and regeneration for organ functioning, all of which provides for an organism's ability to coordinate behaviors conducive to reliable nutrition acquisition and useful habitat modification, where are the wide ontological gaps supposedly dividing mere matter from mentality? If there are such metaphysical chasms, they are not visible to ordinary observation or theoretical science.

Only philosophy persists in that quest for pure ideality untainted by materiality, a quest marked more by theology than anything scientific. That "ghost-like soul entity," as James mocked in *The Principles of Psychology*, was still haunting philosophy, whether it was supposedly marked by substantial consciousness, clear certainty, or transcendent egoism. The pragmatists advanced social psychology over Cartesian individualism, and they were uninterested in elevating humans above animals just to feel closer to angels.

The way that philosophy's idealism still aspired to *scientia* status as knowledge alongside genuine sciences only made the quest more pathetic for the pragmatists. For them, the philosophical ban on teleological explanation, liberating early science from God's grand plan, had to be only a temporary strategy. So long as maturing physical sciences, life sciences, and behavioral sciences were told that they could not believe their own theoretical eyes, they would remain splintered and incomplete, doomed to be incommensurable among each other and incommensurate with the unified Nature in front of them.

This scientific puzzle was extraordinarily convenient for idealizing philosophy and its zealous mission to dictate methodologies and distributing ontological responsibilities to the sciences. Together with spiritualizing theology, philosophy continually denigrated science for failing to explain the mind, and hence the soul. From Descartes to Kant and thereafter, only necessity seemed truly scientific, as lawful as a divine command. The empirical and contingent stayed stubbornly irrational, as distant from God's mind as anything material could be.

Pragmatism, in Process

Resistance against a division of all things rationally necessary from all things irrationally chancy amounts to a rebellion against dualisms of every sort. During the late nineteenth and early twentieth centuries, the physical and life sciences from quantum physics and population genetics were discovering how nature operates in patterned probabilities. Reality is far more statistical than categorical.[4]

Mainstream Anglo-European philosophy and theology largely ignored the sciences for decade after decade during the nineteenth and twentieth centuries, crafting dualism after dualism on an industrial scale. Their dichotomous terminologies were all-pervasive:

subjective / objective, internal / external, intrinsic / extrinsic, essential / accidental, contingent / necessary, a priori/a posteriori, analytic/synthetic, chaotic / lawful, meaningless / meaningful, unfree / free, means / ends, valueless / valuable, fact / value, is / ought, individual / social.

No philosophical or theological issue could be discussed without first classifying matters according to exclusive compartments.

In its rebellion, pragmatism ignored artificed divisions, blended what seemed dichotomous, and synthesized dualities into harmonies and unities. Whatever may be distinguishable in analytic conceptualization may or may not be truly dividable in real actualization. Conceiving two things as separate proves nothing about whether they could persist apart. Only empirical inquiry could be decisive.

Pragmatism sought the eradication of dualism in a naturalism of scientific harmonization by attaining the fulfillment of empiricism in an experimentalism of exploration. A worldview entirely different from dualism is thereby discovered, where the static and separable is replaced by activity and relationality.

Pragmatism, like any worldview philosophy, offers a metaphysics. Rationalism views pragmatism as anti-metaphysical for rejecting their preferred systems. Pragmatism is metaphysical all the same, since displacing poor metaphysics requires good metaphysics. A "non-metaphysical" philosophy lets its own ontological priorities go unquestioned and reinstalls some metaphysics anyways.

A few general tenets can characterize pragmatist metaphysics:

Reality is holistic. Continuities are pervasive throughout all reality. Sharp discontinuity indicates unreality.

Ontology is dynamic. Whatever has actuality is always changing and interactive. Strict fixity marks ideality.

Explanation is contextual. Co-responsive conditions account for the course of processes. Singular causes give approximations.

Learning is creative. New information arises from imaginative and inventive explorations. Assured contentment preserves ignorance.

Knowledge is communal. Improving knowledge requires collaborative experimentation. Subjective certainty protects dogma.

Continuity, Change, Context, Creativity, Community. Substances become situations. Existents become events. Processes are explanatory, in the same way laws are. Organisms are immersed in meaningful values, in the world. Everything known must be learned, not intuited. Cognition is collective, not subjective. Individuality is a learned mode of sociality. Society is constituently codependent, not compounded from independent units. In short, all reality and anything knowable is fundamentally ecological, not atomic or mechanic.

It was Newtonian mechanics and its linear equations that turned out to be the temporary account of the world. Peirce denied the necessary so-called law of mechanics that "every fact in the universe is precisely determined by law" and he doubted that the alleged "law" of conservation of energy is fundamental for cosmology. He sought a "genuine evolutionary philosophy, that is, one that makes the principle of growth a primordial element of the universe."[5] James and Dewey agreed about cosmic growth, and similarly treated mechanistic laws as instrumental conveniences for experimental calculation, not as fundamental forces that precisely dictate a unique future.

Materialism's dim image of dead nature was destined to be just as ghostly as theology's divine creation. That stone-dead materialism, outdated after Maxwell's unification of electricity and magnetism, Darwin's theory of

A "genuine evolutionary philosophy, that is, one that makes the principle of growth a primordial element of the universe."—Charles Sanders Peirce evolution, and the rise of neurological psychology, could no longer stand as the only type of naturalism.

Unfortunately, philosophy and theology maintained their staunch adherence to that Newtonian dogma denying efficacious causation to purpose. Pragmatism decided that Kant was wrong to legislate Newton into God's role: necessary law does not dictate all of nature any more than divine command. Naturalism awaited liberation from divinity in order to do justice to life. Pragmatism completed that liberation, freeing humanity's intelligence to enlarge and enrich this world's opportunities.

Reality is holistic, dynamic, and meaningful, rather than discrete, passive, and valueless. Every academic field and intellectual endeavor must be profoundly affected by that metaphysical reorientation. Peirce, James, and Dewey did not endorse this kind of worldview in order to ground philosophy in science, and they persistently criticized materialism.

Pragmatism would not assign ontology to natural science alone, yet it does align with naturalism in a broad sense, while staying averse to monism, metaphysical dualism, and supernaturalism. A singular ontology, or paired static ontologies, unduly constrain what can and what cannot be developmentally explained. Pragmatism's pluralistic naturalism encourages multiple ontogenies, all engendered within one cosmos. Humanity could not be left incomprehensible within that cosmos. Nothing scientific, for pragmatism, is incompatible with understanding human culture and the human condition.

The pragmatists never imagined that science could, or should, replace philosophy or finally decide answers to central philosophical matters. Philosophy is irreplaceable because a comprehensive worldview integrating all knowledge, a consistent worldview accounting for knowledge of it, and a compelling worldview motivating our participation within it, are perennial projects beyond the competence of the sciences. Philosophy is particularly essential for finding a single worldview satisfying all three projects.

Our knowledge of the world should not displace us from that world or discourage us from caring for that world. The universe depicted by cosmology is coldly indifferent, reducing life to a thin film of seething chemistry coating random planets. Worldviews picturing a quite different cosmos, designed for us and our ambitions, take issue with inconvenient theories such as evolution. Pragmatism sees only unnecessary conflict, faulting both sides for simplifications. Yet simplicities abound. Philosophical rationalism urges a false dilemma of "scientific truth or no truth." Comforting spiritualism counsels a false dilemma of "human value or no value."

Pragmatism steps in here, offering the third option of "scientific knowledge for our values." Knowledge worth pursuing won't be alien to our aspirational goals, and "pure" research today will be essential for technology and society tomorrow. Insulating our values from empirical science is counterproductive; infusing our practices with the experimental attitude brings bountiful results.

Pragmatism, in Practice

Pragmatism is designed to be put into practice across our cultural activities and social institutions. Collaboration with disciplinary knowledge is therefore essential to pragmatist philosophy. Psychology, sociology, anthropology, communications, and education are closely intertwined with pragmatism's development, while those fields have confirmed theories supportive of pragmatist principles. Pragmatism was America's first cognitive science, grounded in evolutionary biology and functionalist neurology. The idea that natural beings are embodying significance and intelligence to some degree or another was a view that came naturally to pragmatists.

A survey of pragmatism's debts to, and influences in, numerous fields of science could begin with logic and computing, such as the invention of the electronic logic machine. Peirce first discovered, in 1880, how Boolean algebra could be expressed via one binary operation, either NAND—not(A and B)—or NOR—not(A or B). Realizing how these basic logical operations could be conducted by electrical switching circuits, he inspired his student Allan

Marquand to design the first electronic logic computer in 1886. Since any logical function can be conducted by some sequence of NAND gates, they constitute all digital control systems, including computers.

During the 1880s, Peirce published his work on quantifiers for the algebra of logic. These ideas were promptly borrowed by Ernst Schröder in his own treatise on the algebra of logic, and then adapted by Giuseppe Peano from Schröder. Peirce also invented three-valued logic, and he was the first to explore the logic of hypothesis or "abduction" to join deduction and induction.[6]

Peirce's establishment of semiotics, or the science of signs,[7] took a further step towards theorizing about the sociality of mentality and the distributed character of information. Norbert Wiener, who studied with William James and John Dewey, inaugurated the field of cybernetics to study dynamical purposive systems.[8] Later pragmatists, such as Hilary Putnam, took close interest in computationalism and its view of brain functioning as information processing.

Regrettably, the key question, about the nature of information for a living organism, was answered most unpragmatically by syntactics and semantic representationalism during the second half of the twentieth century, depicting the human cortex as prefabricated for thinking about beliefs in sentential form. Linguistics proved to be another battleground between pragmatism and the rationalisms of such thinkers as Noam Chomsky and Jerry Fodor, in which language rules are innate and concepts mainly relate to other concepts rather than actions.[9] The original question—how language is about the world—is left a mystery, and the biological evolution of language is rendered inexplicable.

Humans invented speech using a brain already evolving for intense social interaction. Hence, pragmatists sought the basis for communication in the coordination of joint attention during cooperative practices involving material matters. There are numerous broad continuities between animal and human cognition, as would be expected from evolution. Still, human cognition displays some notable discontinuities from animal minds because we evolved further to use both learning and teaching to perpetuate practices as encultured animals. Pragmatism is aligned with theories of the social mind, symbolic interactionism, developmental consciousness, and biosemiotics.[10] It was the primary philosophical foundation for evolutionary theories of "4E Cognition" as embodied, embedded, enactive, and extended. Aspects of connectionism and dynamic systems theory contribute to synthesizing these theoretical standpoints, so long as representationalism is avoided.[11]

The legacy of William James's philosophical psychology enriched many of those later scientific developments. His view of the stream of consciousness, enfolding both internal subject and external object, compelled theories of mind to find confirmations within lived experience. The "self" consists of attachment relations, beyond the body, to one's possessions, shared intimacies with others, and social relationships.[12] Dewey and Mead elaborated on this relational and behavioral self. They argued that the self is originally social, and an individual self emerges from coordinating social roles as personal responsibility emerges later in childhood.

Another line of psychological inspiration from James goes through Edwin B. Holt to James J. Gibson's ecological psychology, explaining how an organism's cognitive abilities are explicable in terms of how that organism exploits environing opportunities.[13] Jakob Johann von Uexküll used the term "Umwelt" for the "life-world" that a species can perceptively engage. Dewey's conception of "experience" as doing–undergoing, Richard Lewontin's environmental constructivism, and Gregory Bateson's ecological cybernetics similarly point to this conception of the available life-world where mentality does its work.[14]

Pragmatism makes a bold stand on a psychological thesis: all thinking functions in an experimental manner, including logicality itself. Psychology and logic can no longer be treated as though they mustn't have anything to do with each other. Logic without relevance is meaningless; thinking without inference is valueless. Pragmatism advocates the experimental method, where social psychology and abductive logic harmonize to attain knowledge.

Experiment, for pragmatism, is no mere intellectual exercise in abstraction detached from concrete existence. Life itself is a grand experiment. A nervous system, in general, continually tries to coordinate sensations with actions for anticipatable results, and a brain continually readjusts activities while monitoring varying conditions in the pursuit of valued goals.

Human brains, while amazingly complex, are no exception. We manage innumerable thoughts by putting them to practical work. Dewey wrote, "Ideas are not then genuine ideas unless they are tools in a reflective examination which tends to solve a problem."[15] Pragmatism is at work within theories of active perception, enactive and extended mind, ecological cybernetics, cognitive anthropology, neurosociology, neurophenomenology, neuropragmatism, and radical embodied cognitive science.[16]

Summary

Today, pragmatism is no longer new, but its characteristic views are getting amply reconfirmed by novel discoveries and rising theories across numerous academic disciplines and scientific fields. Far from an intellectual fad or contemporary fashion, the need for pragmatism will only expand. The greatest age for pragmatism lies more in the future, as its proponents herald revolutionary paradigms for transforming our self-understanding and maximizing humanity's collective potential.

Philosophy itself should be tested by broadening horizons and surprising challenges. Pragmatism expects success with that test, not due to just its own design, but mainly from advising redesigns of many ideas for better serving life. Continually upgrading its application to humanity's concerns, pragmatism offers its practical approach to any area of life.

PERMANENCE AND IMPERMANENCE

Pragmatism opposes any worldview presuming that what changes less has to be more real. For those worldviews, what is most real cannot fundamentally change. That priority of permanence over impermanence sets philosophical agendas for accounts of explanation and knowledge. Having ontological and causal priority, the changeless is necessary to fully explain change, but what changes cannot account for permanence. Pragmatism reverses these priorities, yielding a sounder account of knowledge.

Pragmatism is a philosophy of *impermanence*. Anything real is intrinsically changing—not simply in relations externally, but constituently. What changes less may not be more real, and there is knowledge of reality through change, not despite change. Knowers are dynamic, taking advantage of change within and without to acquire knowledge.

Impermanence does not rule out uniformity; acknowledging some instability inherent to any regularity is far from seeing chaos everywhere. Pragmatism replaces essences with processes and appeals to regular generalities rather than strict necessities. In consequence, natural knowledge discovers how complexities gradually develop from simplicities. The best explanation for something is an account about the processes of its growth.

Being and Plurality

For a philosophy of permanence, knowledge seeks the best explanations, which must refer to what is unchanging. The ultimate goal for knowledge must similarly seek final rest. If the permanent sets the ideal standard for reality, and reality is knowable, then knowledge of reality cannot change.

Real knowledge must therefore be invariant; only invariant knowledge is of something real. Reality is unknowable without any invariant knowledge, so the quest for invariant knowledge is paramount. Knowledge resides with a knower, so the quest seeks knowers of invariant knowledge. People lacking anything invariant about them would not be knowers of invariant knowledge and cannot know reality. A philosophy of *permanence* is thereby established: the changeless supplies the standard for reality, knowledge, and the knower.

As a philosophy of impermanence, pragmatism embraces novelty, temporality, contingency, fluctuation, originality, individuality, development, variety, and plurality. Charles Peirce expresses this affirmation of impermanence as follows:

> Uniformities are precisely the sort of facts that need to be accounted for ... Now the only possible way of accounting for the laws of nature and for uniformity in general is to suppose them results of evolution. This supposes them not to be absolute, not to be obeyed precisely. It makes an element of indeterminacy, spontaneity, or absolute chance in nature.[1]

Pragmatism, liberated from reality conceived as strictly uniform and invariant, embraces reality perceived as discrete, fragmentary, and heterogeneous. William James labeled the prioritization of permanence as "monism" to contrast it with "pluralism":

> The One and All, first in the order of being and of knowing, logically necessary itself, and uniting all lesser things in the bonds of mutual necessity, how could it allow of any mitigation of its inner rigidity? The slightest suspicion of pluralism, the minutest wiggle of independence of any one of its parts from

the control of the totality, would ruin it . . . Pluralism
on the other hand has no need of this dogmatic
rigoristic temper. Provided you grant *some* separation
among things, some tremor of independence, some
free play of parts on one another, some real novelty
or chance, however minute, she is amply satisfied,
and will allow you any amount, however great, of real
union. How much of union there may be is a question
that she thinks can only be decided empirically . . .
Pragmatism, pending the final empirical
ascertainment of just what the balance of union and
disunion among things may be, must obviously range
herself upon the pluralistic side.[2]

Pragmatism cannot see why a degree of indeterminacy
in all things must prevent knowledge. Strict invariance,
the correlate of permanence, is not needed for comprehending the ways of nature, life, or humanity. Both scientific theorizing and human living embody variance and
variety. The exemplification of novelty yields individuality,
as John Dewey asserts:

Individuality conceived as a temporal development
involves uncertainty, indeterminacy, or contingency.
Individuality is the source of whatever is
unpredictable in the world. The indeterminate is

not change in the sense of violation of law, for laws state probable correlations of change and these probabilities exist no matter what the source of change may be.[3]

Several post-Kantian philosophies of impermanence—notably *Naturphilosophie*, life-philosophy, vitalism, existentialism, phenomenology, and process philosophy—have these commonalities with pragmatism. They also prefer concepts and categories acquired from lived experience, as pragmatism does. However, that fidelity to experience displayed by F. W. J. Schelling, Josiah Royce, Martin Heidegger, Alfred North Whitehead, and George Santayana does not suffice for pragmatism. Can mind ever find its rest unless an all-encompassing reality enfolds everything? A reliance on an absolute being, a necessary existence, or an illuminating essence, readymade to forestall reality's dissolution, amounts to a comforting rationalization unconfirmable by experimental inquiries.[4]

Typical allies in impermanence take the world to be a self-sustaining and dynamic realm of ceaseless activity, yet the philosophies of such thinkers as Friedrich Nietzsche, Henri Bergson, Jean-Paul Sartre, and Gilles Deleuze left them short of pragmatism. Philosophies of impermanence are comfortable with partial and perspectival knowledge, yet a disdain for necessities and a prioris is not sufficient.

Recognition for the full reality of diversity, possibility, and individuality is fairly rare across the history of Western thought.

Can the intellect be content with a boundless plurality of independent realms? An embrace of radical multiplicity could not look like the organized cosmos that is known realistically through experimental inquiries.[5]

Pragmatism specifically holds that procedures of experimental learning are constructively engaged with dynamic realities in order to establish valuable objectives of knowledge in the service of successful living. Ideas have no other origin or purpose, and inferences arose from those experimental endeavors too. All the tools and techniques of thinking have themselves developed through past efforts to improve mental attention and control over productive practices.

A pragmatist critique of one of its allies in impermanence would point out how that non-pragmatist philosophy either (a) retains some analog of permanency in its account of reality, knowledge, or value; or (b) refuses to entirely embed cognition and reasoning within normative practices of value. The seductions of permanence and certainty are as perennial as pragmatism's resolute resistance.

Allies are always welcome in a rebellion, but pragmatism directs its efforts towards resisting rationalisms and dualisms due to permanency. A philosophy of permanence requires the objective of knowledge to be static and the means of knowing to be fixed. That pairing of static objects of knowledge with fixed means of knowing makes sense upon prioritizing the permanent. Since the real is invariant, knowing the real cannot alter the real; changing the real cannot be among the capacities of knowing. As for knowledge, knowing cannot alter the means of knowing either. Searching for the invariant around us, and discerning the invariant within us, are the main agendas of philosophies of permanence.

To fulfill those two agendas together, philosophies of permanence diverge into three main strategies: (1) selecting a real invariant first and then finding a means of knowing to match it; (2) selecting an invariant means of knowing first and then defining reality to suit it; or (3) selecting a schema of pure invariance first, and then ensuring that reality and knowing both fit this schema so that reality and knowledge conform to each other.

In the West since ancient Greek philosophy, what is stably real has Being (ontology); knowing rises above change (epistemology); and Reason is the schema for Truth (rationalism). Strategy 1 defines Being first and then designs truthful knowing for discerning the ways of Being. Strategy 2 settles on certain modes of knowing first and then declares that what is known has Being. Strategy 3 sets up Reason as the arbiter of both the modes of knowing and the ways of Being so their matching yields Truth.

Pragmatism draws attention to ways that these strategies—of *ontological*, *epistemological*, and *rationalist* permanence—have perennially contended against each other since the Pre-Socratics. Each one can expose weaknesses inherent to the others, with none gaining advantage over the rest. Their common quest for permanence, and their fixation on knowledge with indubitable certainty, obstructs their aim to explain how human knowledge is possible. Pragmatism gives up that quest for permanence and certainty, showing the way forward towards knowledge without fears of skepticism.

Knowledge and Objectivity

The strategy of *ontological permanence* strives to ensure that the means of knowing can be adequate to the task of discerning Being. What is truly known must be as static as Being, however Being is preconceived to be.

Because Being is settled, two knowers cannot disagree about it, and knowledge must be statically unitary. Any disagreement unsettles a prior preconception of Being, allowing a plurality of conceptions of Being that ontological permanence is supposed to discourage. Questions therefore ensue about how authentic Being should best be conceived.

Such questions may have answers. Before philosophy arose anywhere, mystical, religious, astrological, and cosmological speculation in many civilizations inspired worldviews offering insights into supreme or ultimate reality. Wisdom traditions upholding and teaching those insights about reality offer guidance for properly apprehending it, effectively yielding answers about best conceiving Being. Being remains foundational, so effective insight is oriented towards it. Oriented knowledge is essential to discerning Being.

Explaining the discernment of Being is just a step away from philosophically accounting for knowledge of Being. Going just a single step further, a justification offered for rightly conceiving Being amounts to a selection of a means for knowing Being. The strategy of ontological permanence, asked to justify a foundational conception of Being, easily transitions into the strategy of *epistemological permanence*.

By proceeding from a means of knowing, the strategy of epistemological permanence would preempt questions about discerning Being. Being is fundamentally what is known, and how it is known. Disagreement is just a departure from the right means of knowing. Descriptions of matters beheld by alternative means, even if useful or insightful, fail to apprehend full Being.

Discrepancies among conceptions of Being are understandable, as alternative worldviews sustain their traditional commitments. Yet the right means of knowing never changes. So long as those worldviews remain fixated on their distinctive ontologies, they lack philosophical justification, from an epistemological standpoint.

Ontological strategies and their oriented knowledge are weak competition as well, so long as they lack epistemic justifications. Since epistemological strategies can and do develop, only one can be correct (so they all presume), so a rivalry among them is inevitable.

Epistemological permanence now takes precedence over ontological puzzles. Each epistemological strategy disdains the others, faulting them for failing to apply the right means for correctly apprehending Being. Nothing can supplement or replace right knowledge: knowledge is as permanent as Being, and there is no multiplicity for types of Being, unlike the plurality of things less real than Being. Each of these strategies finds that other strategies have the wrong means of knowing since their objective is not apprehension of real Being, compared to the authentic Being discerned by its own means of knowing. An epistemological strategy thus expects that only its own means of knowledge is objective, for having its correct objective in Being. Although each strategy takes its own knowledge to be uniquely objective, its justification is circular: this is the right means of knowing since it discerns real Being, and that really is Being because this means of knowing apprehends it.

Ontological permanence yields fundamental ontology linked to oriented knowledge, while epistemological permanence offers fundamental ontology and objective knowledge grounded in circular justification. Both strategies require changeless and unitary Being along with rigidly unique knowing. In modern philosophy, this stance received the label of foundationalism.

Pragmatism, as a philosophy of impermanence, attributes change and plurality to reality while respecting multiple and modifiable ways of knowing. Permanence philosophies classify pragmatism as "non-foundational" for failing to acknowledge a unitary real Being or a singular way of knowing. Permanence philosophies hence accuse pragmatism of abandoning authentic Being, knowledge, objectivity, and truth. Pragmatism therefore seems adrift amidst a chaos of appearances, wish-fulfillments, and illusions, while endorsing subjectivity and opinion.

The third strategy of *rationalist permanence* concurs with that negative assessment of pragmatism, but it is no more impressed by ontological or epistemological permanence. Neither ontological nor epistemological permanence satisfactorily adjudicates among rival ontologies and divergent ways of knowing.

The ontological strategy cannot forestall a multiplicity of conceptions of Being and mutates into the epistemological strategy if it tries, while the epistemological strategy cannot uniquely justify a way of knowing without fallacious circularity. Real Being cannot guarantee its reliable apprehension, while justifiable knowledge cannot guarantee its unique objectivity. The strategy of rationalist permanence accordingly attempts to guarantee the universally objective apprehension of authentic Being through a formal schema (usually adapted from dialectical, logical, mathematical, geometrical, or scientific thinking) to mediate between Being and knowing.

The purpose of a formal schema—and attendant forms, essences, necessities, a prioris, and the like—is to align what Being is like with how Being is known, so that humanity apprehends their correspondence in truth. As a strategy of permanence, rationalism appeals to a rigidly formal schema which would not change while directing the acquisition of knowledge.

Rationalist permanence does not have to support its formal schema with another epistemological justification, so no circularity ensues. However, the design of the formal schema must fulfill its purpose of aligning Being and knowing despite the ultimacy of Being and the humanity of knowers. Formal schemas vary in this respect concerning alignment in order to handle possible causes of misalignment and ignorance. Perhaps Being seems less than amenable to apprehension, or humanity seems more interested in distractions than knowledge. What all permanence schemas have in common is a strict invariance for all knowers so they apprehend unitary Being.

In the West, philosophies of ontological and epistemological permanence characterized the Pre-Socratic period, with rationalist permanence flourishing in Plato, Aristotle, and many subsequent philosophies. Dewey laments their denigration of practical know-how:

> If one looks at the foundations of the philosophies of Plato and Aristotle . . . it is clear that these philosophies were systematizations in rational form of the content of Greek religious and artistic beliefs. The systematization involved a purification. Logic provided the patterns to which ultimately real objects had to conform, while physical science was possible in the degree in which the natural world, even in its mutabilities, exhibited exemplification of ultimate immutable rational objects . . . they brought with them the idea of a higher realm of fixed reality of which alone true science is possible and of an inferior world of changing things with which experience and practical matters are concerned. They glorified the invariant at the expense of change, it being evident that all practical activity falls within the realm of change. It bequeathed the notion, which has ruled philosophy ever since the time of the Greeks, that the office of knowledge is to uncover the antecedently real . . . As a form of knowledge it is concerned with the disclosure of the Real in itself, of Being in and of itself. It is differentiated from

other modes of knowing by its preoccupation with a higher and more ultimate form of Being than that with which the sciences of nature are concerned.[6]

Practical activity, for pragmatism, can be no less rationally justifiable than any speculative passivity. Pragmatism also endorses schemas, more empirical and modifiable than formal and invariant, that function to mediate between reality and knowers.

Although pragmatism respects reliable reasoning, invariant reason is problematic. Any schema must be applicable by humans to regulate their means of knowing, including an invariant schema. What, if anything, is invariant about human beings as naturally changing and perishing biological creatures?

A difficult dilemma for a rationalist philosophy looms here, and both options result in *unnatural permanence*. Either the invariant schema is something unnatural within humanity, or the invariant schema is unnaturally separate from humanity. If the former, explaining how humans manage their dual natures is as challenging as explaining knowledge in the first place. If the latter, then the relationship between a natural human and a transcendent schema becomes a mystery.

Rationalist permanence promised objectivity about this world, but it generated invariances beyond this world.

Ensuring that knowledge schemas remain as natural as their objects of knowledge provides the better guarantee that knowledge is humanly attainable. Pragmatism proposes that mediating schemas are created and improved by humanity while exploring and transforming the world, so schemas would not be unnaturally internal or external to the human enterprise. Philosophies of permanence are never impressed by this naturalization of knowledge, complaining that Being and truth are deformed by pragmatism down to a relative dependency upon humanity.

Rationalist philosophies disparage pragmatism for failing to reach the sort of authentic Being and valid truth set up by that preoccupation with permanence. Pragmatism responds with the same complaint against rationalism: Being's permanency separates it from humanity's impermanence, leaving an ontological and epistemological gap unbridgeable by humans.

Pragmatism and rationalism always accuse the other of failing to attain objectivity and truth. Yet they do not mean the same thing by "objectivity" or "truth." For rationalism, objectivity primarily involves an independence from knowers, the aloofness of Being. For pragmatism, objectivity primarily involves a practical achievement of knowers, the accomplishment of knowledge.

That difference in emphasis for objectivity affects what "truth" specifically means. Pragmatism ascribes truth to achievable knowledge of capable knowers. Rationalism attaches truth to infallible knowledge of immutable Being. If rationalism's meaning for truth is pressed upon pragmatists, they abandon that view of truth—along with purified ideas of representation and correspondence—as irrelevant to knowers. If pragmatism's meaning for truth is offered to rationalists, they dismiss that notion of truth—along with practical ideas of experiment and confirmation—as inadequate to reality.

Both pragmatism and rationalism lay claim to objectivity. The amount of human involvement, in comparison to Being's independent contribution, would appear to be the contentious question. But that manner of partitioning responsibility for knowledge between humanity and reality is rationalism's craftwork. What is so divided cannot be easily reunited. For rationalism, the basis to objectivity lies in what is ideally rational, as it mediates between knowers and reality—the real is the rational while the rational sets the ideal standard for what is knowable. Yet rationalism must say whether knowledge of everything real is possible. The affirmative and negative answers both lead to problematic positions.

First, suppose that what is real must be what is ideally knowable. Reality is what exists according to ideal knowledge and nothing real could stay separate from knowers. This supposition is the foundation for metaphysical idealism: reality stably consists of what is ideally knowable, so all knowledge is perfectly concordant through a formal schema.

Although this foundation satisfies the requirement of permanence for reality, metaphysical idealism betrays rationalism's promise to deliver objectivity through reality's independent contribution. Nothing real can make any truly independent contribution, for nothing is real outside of ideal knowing. However, from the perspective of an individual knower, that idealized reality would play an objective role in knowledge, as the absolutely final reality towards which an individual's relatively partial knowing should be aimed. Nevertheless, for this "objective idealism," reality consists only of the ideally knowable.

Second, suppose that what is real can lie beyond what is ideally knowable. But anything so separate from knowledge is intrinsically unknowable and unavailable for contributing to an explanation of how knowledge is attained. Metaphysical realism is the position that reality is independent from knowing it. Yet any knowing only knows what is known: what is known by knowing exists *there* for knowledge, not somewhere *beyond* knowledge. Whether what is known also exists beyond the scope of knowing is a further question, a question that cannot be answered by knowledge. Metaphysical realism therefore demands a non-rational act of faith, the faith that a reality stays identical and unchanged regardless of whether it happens to be accessible for knowing, or inaccessible to knowing.

As a philosophy of permanence, metaphysical realism requires invariant realities to be unaffected by entering into, or passing out of, a relationship with knowing and knowers. With that expectation in place, unalterable reality itself somehow guarantees that all knowledge is perfectly concordant with reality's own structure. However, metaphysical realism provides no way of knowing that reality satisfies that mere expectation beyond the reach of knowledge. As unknown and unknowable, anything beyond knowledge cannot help explain how knowledge is possible, leaving only what exists for knowing.

Although it claims to avoid metaphysical idealism's fate of collapsing reality down to the knowable, metaphysical realism may amount to "subjective" realism: reality is only how it is knowable for knowers. Indeed, subjective realism, in the absence of a guarantee of any knowing-independent reality, collapses further into subjective idealism: the only reality is what is knowable by individual knowers.

Despite pragmatism's reputation for disinterest in realism, realism's rescue proved to lie with the abdication of rationalism and the ascension of pragmatism.

Rationalism and Dualism

From pragmatism's viewpoint, the way that rationalism partitions responsibility for objective knowing between reality and humanity only leads to the abandonment of realism. Metaphysical idealism and metaphysical realism agree that knowledge is attainable, invariant, and concordant. Their disagreement erupts where metaphysical idealism refuses to take it on faith that the real can be thought to transcend knowledge. Metaphysical realism guarantees reality without means to know it; metaphysical idealism guarantees knowledge without a reality to know. What sensible realism is left?

There is a third metaphysical possibility: no reality is knowable, since whatever is accessible to knowers is inconstant, relative, and discordant. This position is occupied by modern skepticism. Unlike ancient skepticism, modern skepticism is metaphysical and rationalistic because it is based on presumptions about what reality would be (permanent, absolute) and what knowledge should be (unchanging, concordant). Although affinities between pragmatism and ancient skepticism can be identified, pragmatism does not recommend contentment with conventional or subjective belief, so hereafter "skepticism" refers only to its modern and metaphysical form. The accusation of skepticism directed at pragmatism by modern competitors usually amounted to a worry over epistemic relativism.[7]

These three rationalisms—objective idealism, subjective realism, and modern skepticism—struggle to classify pragmatism. Pragmatism seems too realistic to idealism, and too idealistic to realism.

Objective idealism worries that pragmatism's disinterest in the absolutely ideally real prevents efforts knowing any unique objective, leaving only ignorant discord, relativism, and perhaps subjectivism. Metaphysical realism cannot respect pragmatism's disinterest in realities transcending all knowing, so subjective idealism appears to be pragmatism's home.

Furthermore, pragmatism's high tolerance for knowledge's mutability seems like relativism and skepticism to both idealism and realism. For its part, metaphysical skepticism could not adopt pragmatism, since pragmatism disdains rigidly ideal standards for knowledge upon which skepticism relies. Rationalisms are incredulous towards pragmatism's avowal to uphold a reasonable realism, so they typically regard pragmatism as a resignation to relativism, subjectivism, and skepticism.

Pragmatism arose during the late nineteenth century, after rationalism took modernist forms. Modern rationalism adapts features of idealism and realism, while continuing to struggle with that dualistic partitioning of responsibility between knowers and reality. To ensure that the unique reality is correctly recognized by all humanity, the same generic schema of reasoning structures each knower's cognition in the manner needed for acquiring knowledge of reality's structure. Individuals may deviate from that strict cognitive path due to less intellectual distractions, allowing their understanding of the world to follow conventional notions perpetuated by social habits—primarily language, ritual, belief customs, and practical ways of life.

Rationalisms since Descartes go by various labels, but the dominant types have been empiricism, transcendentalism, and materialism. Pragmatism was inaugurated and developed during the second half of the nineteenth century and the first half of the twentieth century, a period roughly bracketed by the strong influence of Kant's transcendentalism and Quine's physicalism, with Hegel's absolutism and Mill's empiricism situated in between. From the perspective of pragmatism, all four philosophies are rationalist in form and function. For example, compare Kant and Quine. A singular rational structuring (Kant's categories and schemas, Quine's unity of science program) uniquely organizes the invariant knowledge of the real world (Kant's empirical realism, Quine's reductive physicalism).[8]

Absolute idealism's confidence that the structuring of (dialectical) reason constitutes the essence for the objective world, and empiricism's confidence that the world of perceptual phenomena constitutes the essence of objectivity for the structuring of (inductive) reason, are no less rationalist in spirit. For rationalistic empiricism, clear perceptions caused by the world are combined through conscious rational inferences (refined by logical philosophy) to yield objective knowledge of the world. For transcendentalism, chaotic sensations get structured by preconscious rational schemas, and further reliance on those hidden schemas (discerned by transcendental philosophy) yields knowledge of the objective world. For materialism, objective observations of the world's ways inspire hypothetical reasoning (guided by scientific philosophy) to yield rational knowledge of the world's hidden structure.

Each modern rationalism struggles to explain the basis for its preferred rational schema, beyond taking the characteristic rationalist view that a rigid schema is necessary for objective knowledge.

Rationalist empiricism is hospitable to whatever commonly appears in experience, only asking logical thinking to filter out confusing, biased, and illusory irrelevancies from our attention. Empiricism's traditional weakness was its inability to explain how logic itself is known, since no amount of contingent perception would assemble into logical necessities. (Pragmatist empiricism overcomes that limitation through the pragmatic principle of clear conception and abductive inference.) This incapacity leads to a formal dualism between worldly perception and unworldly logicality, which weakens rationalist empiricism's claim to be the most realistic philosophy.

That presumption of human logicality is transcendentalism's opportunity to refute empiricism and locate logicality in humanity's unworldly reason. However, transcendentalism's weakness is its inability to explain how perception arises, since anything responsible for perceptual appearances must lie beyond the reach of reason and all knowledge. This weakness leads to an ontological dualism between the phenomenal and the transcendental, which weakens transcendentalism's claim to guarantee knowledge of a singular world.[9]

Overcoming that dualism opens the opportunity for objective idealism, which credits a real schema of reason with providing both worldly perception and its organization into knowledge. With absolute reality identified with this rational schema, objective idealism's weakness lies in its difficulties explaining why that absolute final reality would manifest in finite fallible knowers. This weakness leads to a personal dualism compelling a knower to simultaneously and self-contradictorily participate in perfect and imperfect experience.

Admitting that all experience is fallible is the starting place for materialism. Materialism privileges scientific methodology over ordinary perception so that provisional yet confirmable hypotheses permit realistic knowledge about underlying physical reality. The tension between the two worlds that knowers must navigate—one austerely quantitative and the other richly qualitative—is a weakness that leads to a value dualism between a meaningless world and a meaningful world. To overcome that dualism, the common lived world can be restored to its rightful priority over science's dead abstractions, leading to a commonsense empiricism.

And so, this metaphysical cycle returns to rationalist empiricism, without guaranteeing objectivity or preventing dualisms anywhere around the circular track.

Summary

Pragmatists, and philosophies of impermanence generally, share a pessimistic analysis of rationalism and all philosophies of permanence, faulting their obsession with invariance. Pragmatism's ontology respects impermanence, pragmatism is suspicious towards epistemology, and pragmatism rejects rationalism.

Pragmatism distinguishes itself among philosophies of impermanence with a defining set of agendas:

Deprioritizing permanence for reality, knowledge, and human nature.

Denying that simplicity is unable to explain complexity.

Deterring dualisms with continuities, contexts, and potentialities.

Deferring to construction rather than correspondence on knowledge and truth.

Demoting necessities and essences to roles within processes of acquiring knowledge.

Depending on dynamic, systemic, and social relations to explain mentality, learning, and knowing.

Defining all types of meanings in functional and practical ways.

Discerning the purposive and normative in reality.

CONTEXT AND REALITY

Pragmatism has criticized rationalism and the quest for permanence for falling short of objectivity while fostering dualisms, and failing to account for any knowledge worth having. Rationalism in turn accuses pragmatism of avoiding reality and ending up with relativism and irrealism. Relating knowledge's truth to knower's trials accordingly looks like subjectivism and skepticism.

In *Pragmatism*, William James said that a hypothesis is true if it "works satisfactorily in the widest sense of word."[1] Bertrand Russell, who exemplified rationalistic empiricism, summarized its verdict:

> James's doctrine is an attempt to build a
> superstructure of belief upon a foundation of

scepticism, and like all such attempts it is dependent on fallacies. In his case the fallacies spring from an attempt to ignore all extra-human facts . . . this is only a form of the subjectivistic madness which is characteristic of most modern philosophy.[2]

That unfair interpretation had already been anticipated and countered by James in *The Meaning of Truth*. The widest sense of "works satisfactorily" is far more than "has worked well for me personally so far" or "benefits my group more than anyone else." What works well with whatever else is known for anyone and everyone could not be an idea disconnected from hard realities. Science knows of no other meaning for truth. As Albert Einstein said, "Truth is what stands the test of experience."[3]

Knowledge is Constructive

Pragmatism is interested in fruitful engagements with reality, not absorptions into reality or certainties about reality. Like experimental science before it, pragmatism finds enough reality where it can be encountered, explored, and transformed. Pragmatism is a philosophical project of wider scope than scientific investigation, but it has that same spirit of tentative and revisable learning.

In the words of James,

As I understand the pragmatist way of seeing things, it owes its being to the break-down which the last fifty years have brought about in the older notions of scientific truth. 'God geometrizes,' it used to be said; and it was believed that Euclid's elements literally reproduced his geometrizing. There is an eternal and unchangeable 'reason'; and its voice was supposed to reverberate in Barbara and Celarent. So also of the 'laws of nature,' physical and chemical, so of natural history classifications—all were supposed to be exact and exclusive duplicates of pre-human archetypes buried in the structure of things, to which the spark of divinity hidden in our intellect enables us to penetrate. The anatomy of the world is logical, and its logic is that of a university professor, it was thought. Up to about 1850 almost every one believed that sciences expressed truths that were exact copies of a definite code of non-human realities. But the enormously rapid multiplication of theories in these latter days has well-nigh upset the notion of any one of them being a more literally objective kind of thing than another. There are so many geometries, so many logics, so many physical and chemical hypotheses, so many classifications, each one of them good for so much and yet not good for everything, that the notion that even the truest formula may be a human device and not a literal transcript has dawned upon us. We hear scientific laws now treated as so much 'conceptual shorthand,' true so far as they are useful but no farther. Our mind has become tolerant of symbol instead of reproduction, of approximation instead of exactness, of plasticity instead of rigor . . . which at any rate makes our whole notion of scientific truth more flexible and genial than it used to be.[4]

After theology proved unable to justify its faith in an ideally providential order of creation, and science abandoned its parallel search for a perfectly rational order to nature, philosophy began to realize that unitary and static permanence is an inappropriate objective for knowledge of reality. Even mathematical and logical systems no longer pointed to one platonic realm, so postulating an additional formal reality besides natural reality seemed pointless. Any reality for knowing, and worth knowing, actively undergoes modifications and responds to alterations.

Pragmatism agrees with rationalism that knowledge involves *mediation* between known reality and the knower. However, nothing invariant characterizes these three factors, and no dualistic separation divides them. For pragmatism, knowing is a *dynamic coordination* between reality's processes and human endeavors within reality. Knowledge is something that develops within that broad field of human–reality interaction, where controlled explorations—called "inquiries" by pragmatism—are undertaken.

Pragmatism rejects any ontological or epistemic division between what is external and what is internal, a divide elevated into a metaphysical dichotomy by much of modern Western philosophy. Knowers do not have to first ascertain where external reality has to be. The reality amenable for coordination is the environing world in which inquiring knowers are already actively living.

Knowers do not have to predetermine what internal knowing has to be, either. The knowledge achievable through coordination is the result of activity conducted in the environing world by knowers undertaking inquiries. The activities of inquirers occur in congruence with the world's activities, and this common arena of activity situates the capacity for knowing and the enlargement of knowledge.

According to rationalism, the capacity for knowing depends on a fairly stable schema quite unlike the shifting scene of worldly events or the transitory stream of mental thoughts. Rationalism must account for a schema's relationship with the world on the one side and with the mind on the other. When rationalism asserts a correspondence between schema and world, so that there is knowledge in the external sense, it does not have to follow that any human mind is self-aware of this knowledge. An individual could know something without a personal understanding that it is known. For example, a person believing a proposition P that happens to be made true by the world could be said by rationalism to "know P" without appreciating that P is known.

Similarly, when rationalism asserts a correspondence between schema and mind, so that there is knowledge in the internal sense, it does not have to follow that any worldly reality exists in accord with this knowledge. An individual could know something while nothing guarantees that it is real. For example, a person knowing a proposition P that happens to perfectly cohere with other propositions could be said by rationalism to "know P" without any confirmation that any of those propositions are about actual realities.

Some rationalisms admit to skeptical consequences following from these limitations, while other rationalisms instead additionally argue that a knower's adherence to the formal schema ensures that both the state of knowing and the state of reality is appreciated by the knower.

Pragmatism's view of knowledge never requires such extra assurances. Knowers must appreciate their possession of knowledge since their inquisitive efforts construct it, and knowers must appreciate the reality known because their inquiries engage with it. No veridical knowledge is first required for the knower to encounter reality and constructively engage with it.

Inquiry's methods of exploration are sophisticated and thoughtful versions of ongoing habitual activities already embedded within reality, where knowers are engaging with the world. Most of what is encountered is never known, and there is more to knowable reality than what gets encountered. Inquiries only directly deal with what is encountered (whether as known or not known) yet inquiries indirectly deal with what is not encountered (which may become known).

Pragmatism insists that what becomes knowable beyond the familiar arena of worldly engagement, such as unobservably past events, invisibly tiny entities, and cosmically vast forces, must have dynamic relations with matters occurring within the encounterable arena.

Reality is Effective

Pragmatism's commitments to holism, dynamism, and contextualism help to explicate its approach to knowable realities. This philosophy of impermanence prioritizes interdependency and functionality, rather than substantiality or inherency, for all ontologies. Existing beings have no essence, no rigid character, defining what they must be.

An "essence" as a permanent nature assigning a thing to a kind necessarily, once and forever, is only an imaginative postulation, unable to ontologically refer to anything exemplified in reality. Conceiving an essence relies on the predication of static attribute(s)—qualities, properties, traits, and so on—to an entity unable to exist without them or to modify them. Static attributes for fixed entities have no place in pragmatist ontology.

Sciences do utilize formulas expressing necessary relations among theoretical matters (such as "mass" and "energy"), and pragmatism admits their candidacy for ontological existence as powers and forces so long as necessary relations do not exhaust conceptions of them. An item of pure theory entirely defined by necessary relations (such as mathematized formulas or equations) represents a preliminary stage of inquiry at most, awaiting a clearer conception about effects and consequences per the pragmatic maxim.[5]

The notion of essence is replaceable by "process" without any detriment or deficit to knowing natural entities. The proposition "S is P" hides a metaphysics of permanence in its grammar; "This Process has Attribute" is preferrable, or "This P has A" for brevity. In order to "predicate" an attribute functionally, rather than substantially, a selected stability (not a fixity) about an ongoing process is picked out for its connectivity with some other stability to yield further processes.

Attribution is a triadic relation of context, involving a process, an attribute, and its capacity. To say that "a rose has redness" is to choose a feature of a rose for its availability to visual appreciation. To say that "a plant has roots" is to choose a feature of a plant for its connectivity to accessible nutrients (water, nitrogen, minerals, etc.) held by soils. To say that "a soil has moisture" is to choose a feature of a soil for its capacity to yield water. To say that "water is wet" is to choose a feature of an amount of water for its partial transferability to another surface on contact (that is why a single molecule of water cannot be "wet"). To say that "a water molecule has polarity" is to choose a feature of H_2O for its tendency to orient the oxygen atom towards any positive magnetic charge.

Does science at last reach essences? The definition of H_2O as "two protons in electron bonds with an oxygen atom" cannot identify a fixed essence, since a group of water molecules in nature rapidly redistribute their electrons. Molecules are dynamic processes, and so are atoms and all subatomic particles—with fluctuating wave-function fields describing them—in accord with expectations of pragmatism and process philosophy.[6]

Bringing up "redness" or "wetness" invites two challenges to this process ontology. A perceptual quality like "red" invites the accusation of subjectivism, while a physical property like "wet" raises the worry of irrealism.

Why can't the red quality really inhere in the rose, the accusation goes, rather than within the perceiver looking at the rose? Pragmatic contextualism replies by denying that colors only exist with either object surfaces, or lighting, or reflectance spectra, or retinal stimulation, or perception. Colors evidently depend on many contextual factors and hence colors objectively exist where they can appear, within situations that include all factors.[7] (This situational analysis applies to more than "phenomenal" qualities; pragmatism treats "meaning," "value," and "information" in the same manner.)

A physical property such as wetness can seem less real than a color, if standards of permanence are applied. If water isn't actually wet all the time, and the wetness isn't within a perceiver either, it must somehow enter and depart existence instead of having its own reality, leading to irrealism. Should we worry about irrealism? Pragmatism does not have to resort to subjectivism or irrealism. Supposing that "deeper" fixed properties ground relational capacities and dispositions, or proposing that dispositional powers are fundamental, is the tactic of a permanence metaphysics.

Deeper properties to things there may be, but they will be no less contextual, so, those subjectivist and irrealist anxieties due to permanence linger "all the way down." Relief comes from abandoning the metaphysics of permanence and its insistence that reality is marked by fixity and independence. The real is interactive and effective.

Pragmatism replaces the traditional primacy of subject–predicate relations with structure–function relations.

Stabilities taken for their connections presently are the structures; those connections taken for their development temporally are the functions. Neither structure nor function can persist without the other; structures are always functioning and functions are always structuring—they are two ways of regarding complex processes from either spatial or temporal perspectives. Scientific investigations can focus on one or the other depending on the purposes of inquiry, but science ultimately regards "space-time" as unified.

Isolating a notion of some sort of "static" structure that does nothing somewhere, or some kind of "generic" function that might manifest anywhere, is only an imaginative exercise without exemplification in reality. Reverting to previous illustrations, neither "red" nor "wet" by themselves torn out of situational contexts can refer to anything actual. Seeking something, anything, to anchor their references is a hopeless task for permanence metaphysics. It is unnecessary to suppose that "red" is an idea due to abstracting out a static commonality from many perceptions, or that "wet" is conceived by distilling out a rigid causality among many correlations.

Taking matters in their interdependencies will yield clear conceptions, while aloofness and isolation leads to meaninglessness. Ontology goes no "deeper" than structure–function processes. That pragmatist manner of treating ontology calls for a reorientation of the meta-physical enterprise of ontological priority.

For the metaphysics of permanence, one thing has ontological priority over another if the first thing persists while the second stops existing. Whatever has the highest ontological priority, by surviving the most comparisons, is the "most real" and substantial. Light is prior to a shadow it casts, atoms are prior to the rock they compose, and so on.

Pragmatism sees how this test of ontological priority fails for both mechanical and biological entities. There is no sense to asking, "which existed first, the screw or the screwdriver?" or "which could exist without the other, a stomach organ or a mammal?" That puzzling game of asking, "But which had to come first?" is no longer a productive way of asking nature about what it has been doing.

As science amply discovered during its maturation, ontological priority no longer has a regulative or explanatory role. In an endlessly dynamic world, a thing capable of causing change in something else must already be undergoing a process of change, too. Dewey wrote,

> There is no action without reaction; there is no exclusively one-way exercise of conditioning power, no mode of regulation that operates wholly from above to below or from within outwards or from without inwards. Whatever influences the changes

In an endlessly dynamic world, what is capable of causing change in something else must already be undergoing a process of change, too.

of other things is itself changed. The idea of an activity proceeding only in one direction, of an unmoved mover, is a survival of Greek physics. It has been banished from science, but remains to haunt philosophy.[8]

Pragmatism's pluralistic ontology diffuses reality across endless connectivities and contexts, without anything playing the role of "the most real." In a dynamical cosmos, everything can affect something else and nothing lasts unaffected.

Emergence is Creative

To illustrate this dynamical pluralism, consider debates among naturalists over "emergence." The term "emergence" is nowadays overused, while allied with the reductionist agenda of physicalism. For "part-to-whole" emergentism, an individual part has its own rigid properties/powers to exhibit independently from wholes (the reductionism) while a whole's properties remain entirely dependent on its particular parts (the emergentism). This sort of "bottom up" emergence begs the question in its presumption that parts are more real than their wholes, so it cannot be a genuine alternative to reductionism, but only its restatement.

Part-to-whole emergentism commits the analytic fallacy: a decomposition to discriminate a "component" in isolation, so external relations are required to get it to operate with other components. To avoid this fallacy, do not presume that (a) a component existed prior to decomposition or that (b) external relations were at work prior to decomposition. Whether (a) or (b) might be accurate for any particular matter is subject to empirical inquiry. A top–down emergentism is not reductionistic, but it would be just as fallacious, rashly presuming prior to evidence that (c) a whole existed prior to composition or that (d) internal relations were at work prior to composition.

Pragmatism, by contrast, finds that parts emerge from wholes as much as wholes emerge from parts, depending on developing contexts. Sometimes new properties of a whole arise from configurations of its parts. Sometimes new properties of parts arise from developments by the whole. Let "emergence" be about a whole's attributes that do depend on parts. Pragmatism equally well recognizes "demergence" about a part's attributes that depend on the whole. In other words, both synthesis and analysis are creative processes. Taking a whole apart creates new attributes of resulting parts they lacked before analysis, just as assembling a whole creates new attributes from parts that it lacked before synthesis.

Creativity in a dynamically interrelated and ecological cosmos is always unavoidable. Both analysis and synthesis involve dramatic alterations of context. To insist that "a part must have the same properties unchanged before and after its participation in a whole" has no more validity than "a whole must have the same properties unaltered before and after its constitution by parts."

Put another way, it is all about the conditioned emergence of novelty no matter how contexts are altering. The related notion of "supervenience" to explain how a complex whole displays novel attributes that are somehow less real or quite unreal can be similarly discarded. Nor does contextualism have to heed warnings about "causal overdetermination" since there is no level or scale of reality where some exclusively "real" causality is entirely responsible for all change. Causal perspectivism in step with multiple ontologies is the sounder scientific approach.[9]

In philosophy of mind, pragmatism rejects permanence presuppositions needed for phenomenalism and epiphenomenalism. Later chapters discuss pragmatism on the topic of mind. In philosophy of science, pragmatism rejects similar assumptions at work in the program of reductionism. Reductionism assumes that entities discovered at the smallest discrete scales must also exist at any other size and energy scale everywhere in the cosmos. Reductionism relies on a universalist view of natural laws, because the laws for those minimal (subatomic) levels must prevail everywhere as well, and nothing else can occur anywhere without the involvement of those laws. Reductionism amounts to an overexaggerated and unnecessary realism.[10]

Pragmatism offers "productionism" instead: entities discovered through controlled experimental conditions really exist, whenever and wherever those conditions happen to prevail anywhere in the cosmos.

Pragmatism denies universalism about natural laws, since there is no evidence that laws operating under certain conditions are prevailing anywhere else in the cosmos in dissimilar conditions. Productionism is contextual scientific realism: theorized entities (whether particles, forces, fields, and so on) really exist where modeled conditions required for their existence happen to prevail, such as in controlled experiments or elsewhere in nature where similar conditions produce them without intelligent control.

Subatomic particles detected in supercolliders are fully real, just as they were real in the earliest seconds of the Big Bang or under the extreme conditions within supernovas or near black holes. But there is no logical or scientific justification for assuming that nature takes those forms under quite different conditions, such as those prevailing on planets. There are no quarks present in the tip of my finger, nor are laws governing quark behavior describing anything occurring inside my body. Other theoretical entities from electrons to endorphins are realistically present on earth, as described by physics, chemistry, and physiology under temperature and pressure conditions at planetary surfaces.

Reductionism misplaces ontological priority upon parts, not because wholes are more real, but because reductionism, like philosophies of permanence generally, forgets the crucial role of *conditioning context*. For the pluralism of impermanence, ontological *priority* is replaced by ontological *parity*: so long as something is clearly (pragmatically) conceived, it may be just as real as anything else credibly discovered.

Labelling certain sorts of things as "more real" only calls attention to human preferences and values. Neither smallness nor bigness, neither locality nor universality, and neither transience nor ubiquity, make anything more or less real, according to ontological parity. Science cannot disagree. Cosmology and physics, for example, exhibit such parity. Galaxies are not more real than atoms, since stars formed from atomic condensations, while atoms are not more real than galaxies, because galactic evolution created atoms heavier than oxygen.

Another corollary to a pragmatic process ontology is "real modalism"—the reality of dynamic generalities. Not to be confused with "modal realism" in which a proposition's possibility is made true by an actual world among innumerable equally existent worlds, "real modalism" takes the truth of modal propositions to rest on a multiplicity of generals existing in this one world. To say that "a rock necessarily falls when dropped" isn't to think that all worlds of possible rocks have fallings from droppings, but only to say that *this* actual world has a generality of unsupported falling rocks. An ontology of real generals depicts this actual world as one of innumerable interrelated regularities. Nature has habits.

On Peirce's pragmatic maxim, conceiving the reality of thing calls for conceptions of its potencies for detectible effects at any time under certain contexts. Real things exhibit habits of activity extending indefinitely both backwards and forwards in time. This realism, central to the pragmaticism of his later philosophy, is only recommended but not determined by induction, since real habituality surpasses any finite amount of observation. (That is why no "problem of induction" derails the productive realism of pragmatism.)

Peirce asserts that "pragmaticism could hardly have entered a head that was not already convinced that there are real generals."[11] These are not static universals or rigid forms; their role is to be "physically efficient" at most.[12] They do not depart from existence in the absence of activating conditions; their persistent reality explains why conditions can activate consequences. In Peirce's words again, "there are, in a Pragmatistical sense, Real habits (which Really would produce effects, under circumstances that may not happen to get actualized, and are thus Real generals)."[13]

Real generals are neither strict universals nor chancy possibilities. They account for the applicability of universal propositions, such as "trees always grow leaves in the spring" or "tin melts at 449°F." Real generals also explain the accuracy of statistical probabilities—for example, "more than 60% of 65-year-old Americans today will reach age 80" or "the typical fruit fly lives for 14 days." Real generals are neither strict necessities nor uncaused chances, but rather their combination: a stable regularity that inherently deviates from strict necessity.

Scientific fields use formulaic laws for precise calculations of experimental consequences, but their universality is grammatically deceptive. When physics says, "An electron has a charge of –1" it is only saying, "If something is an electron, then it carries a –1 charge," and the question of whether any electron actually or potentially exists is left indeterminate by this hypothetical proposition. Universality does not bear the burden of actuality.

Potentiality and actuality are rooted in ongoing potency, which is perpetually realizing (dynamically *be-ing*). Nothing is static, entirely passive, or suspended in mere possibility. At the very least, something *be-ing* has potency enough to forestall a lapse into non-being. Potentiality is realizable potency; actuality is realized potency.

Possibility and necessity are conceptual classifications, characterizing links of inductive and deductive inference, but they lack exemplification in actuality by themselves.

To be, it is sufficient to be able to make a difference to something else. Sheer necessity, like mere possibility, may lend the appearance of accountability, yet it offers no efficacy, or explanatory power, and cannot be responsible for a single fact.

The Real (ontological):
potentialities–actualities–eventualities.

The Conceptual (logical): possibilities, contingencies, necessities.

Potentialities, actualities, and eventualities find creations, confluences, and compatibilities, as the course of the cosmos proceeds. Possibilities, contingencies, and necessities set negations, contradictions, and incompatibilities, as the course of thought proceeds. When thought collides with an impossibility, thinking must change course, not reality.

As a corollary to pragmatism's accounting for ontological/logical distinctions, it cannot accept strict determinism in reality, although pragmatism does expect all actualities to have conditioning causes. A further corollary to pragmatic process ontology and its real modalism is the tenet that complexity can be explained by simplicity in interactivity plus time, yielding creativity. Nature's vitality is visible in creative growth. Real generals themselves undergo development like any sustained process.

Complexity evidently arises from simplicity. The rival tenet, that complexity can only be explained by complexity, was enshrined in Western philosophy by Anaxagoras, Socrates, and Plato, and then endorsed by Christian theologians crediting a supreme Mind with all creation. The resulting "argument from design" lingered long enough to mistakenly contradict Darwinian evolution.

Summary

Knowing is an achievement principally of active exploration and inquiry, not passive perception or mere cognition. Knowledge, for pragmatism, therefore occurs within that constructive arena of human–reality interaction, not entirely on reality's side (as if the mediation of knowing is primarily external) or on humanity's side (as if the mediation of knowing is primarily internal). Taking mentality and its ways of knowing to be contextual is only a halfway step towards pragmatism, leaving knowledge mired in relativism.

Realities themselves exist interdependently and contextually. Allowing that the mind works contextually while expecting the world to work mechanically only renders knowledge a mystery. For pragmatism, the dynamic coordination of knowing occurs in the same world of activity where all other life functions are already encountering the world.

In a dynamic world, creativity is no mystery. Peirce agreed with Darwin that complexity is precisely what needs explanation more than simplicity. He and other pragmatists treated a chemical process, a living organism, an individual, a mind, a society, a culture, and anything else as the product of developmental growth. Supposing that simplicity always exists before any complexity, or expecting complexity to just appear without development, or imagining how final complexity must be hidden within development, drifts into unscientific speculation.

Explanations for natural knowledge do not need to aim at eliminating indeterminacy or impermanence. Accounts ignoring developmental histories while prescribing necessities are the abstractions that fall short of sufficient explanation.

TRUTH IN CONSEQUENCES

Permanence philosophies adopt a "retrospective" view of truth. Real things should be known, as they are antecedent to knowing. The real cannot be other than exactly what it is, so right thinking about reality must approach that exactitude. Mutability in thinking about something immutable is a mismatch, to be reduced as much as possible for gaining knowledge. Changing matters, so plentiful for perception, keeps thought in flux and minds distracted by practical pursuits, but minds unfocused and disunited will not acquire knowledge.

Unwavering unity, that mark of permanence, serves as the essence of knowing. Right thinking aims at this ideal rectitude of strictest conformity with the real's own unity. The real is surely related to true knowledge of it, without destabilizing that rectitude of thought. Thinking rightly must therefore appreciate reality's independence from mentality while seeking signs that thoughts are relating to realities.

James well understood the challenge of thinking rightly, particularly about two matters, thoughts and things, that must be akin yet distinct. He wrote,

> Truth, as any dictionary will tell you, is a property of certain of our ideas. It means their "agreement," as falsity means their disagreement, with "reality." Pragmatists and intellectualists both accept this definition as a matter of course. They begin to quarrel only after the question is raised as to what may precisely be meant by the term "agreement," and what by the term "reality," when reality is taken as something for our ideas to agree with. In answering these questions the pragmatists are more analytic and painstaking, the intellectualists more offhand and irreflective. The popular notion is that a true idea must copy its reality.[1]

Pragmatism also expects realities to relate to thoughts and hence resolve the challenge of knowledge. Reality is fluctuating, pluralistic, holistic, interdependent, and dynamic. In response, thinking rightly will be flexible, perspectival, non-dualistic, contextual, and anticipatory. Realities and mentalities have the same basic character, so knowing is not radically different from the rest of practical thinking. Knowledge arises from the ongoing interrelationships of mentality with reality. Realities participate in their discovery, not in a retrospectively passive manner, but in a prospectively active manner.

Minds at Rest

A philosophy of permanence explains knowledge in terms of right thinking about realities relating to thoughts. How does thinking understand that its thoughts are rightly relating to realities? Permanence is the needed sign. Knowledge must share in the true character of the real in its permanence, and the real lacks multiplicity or mutability, so the path to knowing must eliminate vagueness, variability, and variance in thinking. Two thoughts cannot match the same real thing so long as they differ from each other. There wouldn't be discordant truths about a real thing, so plurality and perspective are deficiencies, deviations from the truly real, despite the way that attention to variability is conducive to practical mentality.

Knowledge in itself is not variable. To say that "knowledge changes" only points to modified knowledge in a mind keeping up with reality, not that truth changes for each mind. Besides, a philosophy of permanence insists, how could change satisfy a curious intellect seeking the real? Whatever is really responsible for change cannot itself be changing, lest change go unexplained, so thinking must find its own rest in conceptual stasis to know the real. Thinking rightly amidst the mental cacophony of mutable thoughts is an intellectual challenge calling for the regulation of concepts. Regimenting concepts, giving them strict bounds to eliminate vagueness and vagary, guides thinking towards that defined and determined uniformity that characterizes the real's own unity.

A philosophy of permanence aligns with rationalism as a theory of knowledge. A rationalist philosophy seeks what is changeless in the mind so that thinking can apprehend the real. Seeking the changeless in a mind already overflowing with cascading and confluent thoughts calls for strenuous concentration. Flow and flux find relationality in full force, as the suggestivity of one meaning beckons the next and the next, and so on without cessation. Structural relations between thoughts and things is knowledge's aim, not substantial relations among fusing and fissioning thoughts.

Where can a mind come to a full stop on something specially stable? All thoughts are not created equal. A singular idea or concept, whatever its origin known or unknown, must be statically beheld for mental assessment. By conceiving just that concept distinctly and clearly, without taint from unnecessary relations or contrary notions, the mind becomes free from error and deception. Permanence in unity is now paired with conception in purity. Rationalism's core notion of truth is conveyed by this primal co-unity. The mind possesses truth by ensuring that the object of its conception is just that concept itself, rather than something different.

For rationalism, thinking rightly deals in true conceptions. Abstractions liberated from specificities of temporality, spatiality, perspective, and personality may pass that stringent test. That is why only what is general and universal could be fully real for rationalism, leaving anything particular or individual in an unreal or dependent condition. As James explains,

> Rationalism is comfortable only in the presence of abstractions. This pragmatist talk about truths in the plural, about their utility and satisfactoriness, about the success with which they "work," etc., suggests to the typical intellectualist mind a sort of coarse lame second-rate makeshift article of truth. Such truths are not real truth. Such tests are merely subjective. As against this, objective truth must be something non-utilitarian, haughty, refined, remote, august, exalted. It must be an absolute correspondence of our thoughts with an equally absolute reality. It must be what we *ought* to think, unconditionally.

The conditioned ways in which we *do* think are
so much irrelevance and matter for psychology.
Down with psychology, up with logic, in all this
question![2]

Anything particular, relational, perspectival, contingent, or variable cannot participate in a valid conception, so such a thing must be more illusory than fully real. Whatever minds think they encounter through perceptions from the bodily senses cannot be real in their own right, unless and until rational concepts regiment them into such schemas as categorized classes and lawful necessities. Only the purest ratiocination of strict reasoning ensures knowledge's conformity with the unitary and permanently real.

Rationalism took its fully modern form by divesting from anthropology and psychology. Studying whatever many minds happen to unreasonably think about their worlds is relegated to anthropological psychology; studying what the rational mind must logically think about reality is the province of philosophy.

On that rationalist basis, empiricism can either limit itself to the phenomenal (unreal) realms of human belief and all the causes of folly and error, or empiricism can merge into rationalism by allowing pure concepts and prior (a priori) categories to dictate what counts as acquired knowledge of the world. Empiricism kept insisting that perception and its basis in original sensation, when aggregated through congruent association, accumulated into plenty of knowledge. In response, rationalism kept demanding degrees of consistency and coherence that no amount of aggregated sensations could deliver.

Sensationalism, associationism, and positivism from Thomas Hobbes and John Locke to J. S. Mill and Rudolf Carnap never surmounted that challenge. Various strategies to covertly insert conceptual structure into perceptions have been proposed, so that observations would be ready for propositional and inferential roles. Rationalists demanded the same preconceptions for perception, of course, especially because the idea that thinking is instead caused and controlled by material sensation was intolerable for denying freedom to the mind. How could sensory impingements from objects be responsible for, or be held responsible to, beliefs about those objects? The more that empiricists insisted that perception has to cause concepts to form, the more that rationalists insisted that the mind alone must make perceptions meaningful.[3]

The Kantian demand for percept–concept cooperation only states the terms of this tension, without resolving it. Idealists next noticed how that tension is relievable if the external world bears no responsibility for meaning and a singular storehouse of concepts governs all reasoning. This is an idealism crediting a super-mind, an Absolute mind, for all knowledge. Human minds are included within this Absolute, borrowing concepts from its ideal schema in order to make particular judgments as they participate in cognition like cells within an organ.

The twentieth-century "linguistic turn" taken by ordinary language philosophy was absorbed into that rationalist–empiricist conflict, and it soon reinvented idealism. Dismissive towards idealism for its misuse of language's evident ability to make reference to the external world, analytic philosophy chose the proposition as the fundamental unit to bear truth. What makes a proposition true? If a mere perception couldn't even cause the mind to apply the correct concept for it, no perceptions could ever compel an entire proposition to be credible. Look out a window—how many propositional beliefs should be impressed upon one's mind within a 10-second gaze? The epistemological problem of foundationalism and its quest for original observations of worldly truths cannot answer a simple question that its own theory raises.

Analytic philosophy, as a phase of post-Kantian philosophy, instead placed complete responsibility for credible belief on the mind's own activity, where a belief's only credible support comes from other beliefs. This "space of reasons" insulates rationality from causality, which comported well with analytic philosophy's truce with scientific naturalism, leaving the world without norms, values, or meanings anyways. The complete burden of all rationality was placed upon language alone, where no individual minds could have a single cogent thought without consulting common sense, including the sensible minds of philosophers.

Robert Brandom concisely describes this sort of reduction of rationality and logic to a branch of linguistics:

> By "the linguistic turn," here I mean putting language at the center of philosophical concerns and understanding philosophical problems to begin with in terms of the language one uses in formulating them. But there is a more specific significance one can take language to have. By "lingualism" (compare: "rationalism") . . . I shall mean commitment to understanding conceptual capacities (discursiveness in general) in terms of linguistic capacities.[4]

This position amounts to linguistic idealism. Language substitutes for the transcendental super-mind as the common storehouse of applicable concepts available for credible judgments capable of being true or false.

Philosophy now had to ponder, "Which language?" The answer of "God's own language" was no longer an option for secular philosophy. Could logic or syntactics serve instead? No, reference to an external world beyond the sphere of language requires semantics, just as science needs more input than mathematics. However, expecting all intellectual problems to be askable and answerable in English exposed the parochialism of analytic philosophy.

Having reintroduced one social science, linguistics, back into philosophy, others followed. Anthropology could support cultural relativism about human knowledge. "Experimental" philosophy could tell what to think about free will or moral judgment by the sort of group polling done in sociology. Sociology could explain science's paradigms in terms of power structures within scientific fields. Psychology could chart the bounds of one's subjective world by the extent of one's personal vocabulary. Intuitions of philosophers pumping up their arguments was yet another appeal to conformity and familiarity.

Rationalism devolving down to linguistic relativism soon degenerated into skepticism all over again. Linguistic rationalism holds that thinking rightly amounts to thinking coherently along with all other human thinkers using the same language. Whether you are able to know something depends only on the available reasons already affirmed by the vast mass of language users. One can know whatever others think they know too, but is this really knowledge, anywhere?

As the coherentist theory of epistemology well understands, any set of beliefs achieving internal coherence may or may not accurately represent what the external world is really like. The Flat Earth Society can recount its worldview on a pamphlet without stating two beliefs in contradiction. Empiricism has a point: the actual world has to somehow make a credible difference to belief, too. Linguistic coherentism is a schematic idealism that arouses skepticism. It all comes back to the real issue: What concepts should we be using to better understand the world?

By all means agree that concepts sophisticated enough for reasoning are expressible in human language. The corollary is also accurate, that language is adaptable for the reach of human conceptualization. Since language should answer to the development of concepts and learning, and not the other way around, philosophy can refocus on intelligent cognition rather than just linguistics.[5] All talk but no action would leave a species pretty speechless. Language as the preeminent tool for coordinating responsible practices should answer directly to worldly engagements. By comparison, schematism about concepts only dealing with other concepts does not prevent skepticism about knowledge, so some sort of practical empiricism remains indispensable.

Confronted with that dilemma, of skepticism or schematism, empiricism must address the fundamental issue: what is thinking, rightly? Accused of disregarding clarity for cacophony and abandoning truth for wanton opinion, empiricism cannot allow rationalism to define the nature of reasoning itself. Reasoning deals in conceived ideas—what kinds of conceptions are best?

The heart of rationalism must be challenged, and pragmatists did not miss that target. Even if a mind concentrated upon a distinctively clear idea successfully avoids an erroneous thought, that mind gets trapped in its own fixation without intending anything else, other than this present luminous conception. The reality of that conception is admissible, but nothing more.

Anticipating this objection, that a mind at rest is a mind enraptured by itself, rationalism postulates that all distinct conceptions do intend something else, so the mind is simultaneously thinking about a conception and its intended object. This "intentionality" to conceptions cannot amount to any knowledge about the reality of that object, however, since one's conception of the conception and one's conception of its object are mentally identical. One might as well try to verify the accuracy of an old memory by remembering it again the next day. Pragmatism is unimpressed by appeals to the "self-evident," "self-explanatory," and the like. Why should any idea radiate its truthfulness without borrowed light?

Examples of "a priori" propositions offered by rationalists only seem indubitable among those already in agreement about knowing and using particular concepts, an agreement which rationalists cannot explain without abandoning the point of self-illumined concepts.[6] Pragmatism does not seek a final rest upon certainties or stoppages of thought; at most, cognition finds temporary rests and reliefs from doubt. Satisfactory ideas allow for working beliefs, but only because they are presently going unquestioned, not because they are unquestionable. Conceptual truths and analytic propositions get abandoned when they prove unworkable and irrelevant. While a statement radiates its own truth today, a following generation will find it inapt, otiose, or meaningless.

Pragmatism learns the lesson: substantial relations make something real, not its own self-contained or self-sustained isolation. A monadic unity to a conception goes nowhere; a dyadic mirroring of a conception gets nowhere real. Neither purity nor tautology are interesting marks of truth. More should be expected from thinking rightly, if thinking reaches reality.

Concepts at Work

Dynamic thinking must reach farther than frozen or fixated mentality. In Peirce's terminology, what is needed is a triadic account of conceptions, and hence a triadic theory of thinking, inference, and reasoning.

James was ever-ready to credit Peirce for formulating the key principle of reason itself, a rule of clear thinking, in Peirce's "How to Make Our Ideas Clear" from 1878: "Consider what effects, that might conceivably have practical bearings, we conceive the object of our conception to have. Then, our conception of these effects is the whole of our conception of the object."[7]

James expressed Peirce's pragmatic maxim in his own book *Pragmatism*:

To attain perfect clearness in our thoughts of an object, then, we need only consider what conceivable effects of a practical kind the object may involve—what sensations we are to expect from it, and what reactions we must prepare. Our conception of these effects, whether immediate or remote, is then for us the whole of our conception of the object, so far as that conception has positive significance at all.[8]

Notice the core features of their pragmatic principle: (a) a conception must have an object, (b) that object must have conceivable effects, and (c) those conceivable effects must be able to make some sort of difference to our practical activities.

Only this threefold relationality of a clear conception about "object–effects–evidence" allows cognition to think clearly about something real, opening up an opportunity to realize a thing's reality. *An idea of something ineffective is empty; a search for something undifferentiable is blind.* By attending to practical matters, no mind could ever be lost in complete falsity, even if knowledge at best comes in degrees. Mentalities are always somewhere anchored in realities, with intelligible realities always somehow accessible to intelligences. The spectre of skepticism that haunted Europe is dispelled by the modesty of pragmatism.

On Peirce's principle, realism is not abandoned, but rescued. Realities remain central to genuine conceptions.

Conceiving something without effects is to ponder something lacking reality. (Only mathematics deals in such conceptions, as nothing real is intended or implicated, or needed to account for mathematical truth.) Conceiving something only in definitional terms may intend to refer to something, but it does not assert any reality. For example, thinking about how "every body must have extension" does not require the actual existence of any physical bodies or extended things.

Proposing that a conception is realizable on Peirce's conditions is unlike asserting that a proposition is representational. Sustaining a proposition in one's thoughts lets one imagine how a similarly static arrangement exists in reality, but a mere representation never guarantees realization nor provides a sure way to confirm its truth. A genuine conception is instead a dynamic modeling about a possibly real thing participating in the process of its realization for confirmation. This conceptual model consists of potential instructions for experimentally realizing its actuality.

A conception passing Peirce's clarity test is triadic in multiple senses, explored by his semiotics or theory of signs. Three features are essential for a revitalized empiricism in the hands of Peirce and James, and further developed by Dewey.

First, a clarified conception is *our* conception since the psychology of right thinking is communal, not solipsistic, where multiple thinkers are jointly thinking about reality.

Lone thinkers are either arranging thoughts for dialogue or amusing themselves in reveries; even Cartesian meditations use a public language for public understanding. This communality to mentality is emphasized in *social psychology*.

Second, a clearly consequential conception of something lends itself to processes of inferential thinking automatically, without supplemental abstract premises. Chains of meaningful implications are built into all conceptions worth thinking about, since objects have conceived effects, and those effects must have conceivable implications for other matters, and so on, endlessly. Mentality's endless enchainment in sequences and syntheses inspires *semiotics*.

Third, thinking rightly for knowing must predict empirical consequences, plan out differentiable conditions, and thereby confirm experimental results. Unlike deduction's validities or induction's probabilities, such thinking requires abduction's hypotheses about possible realities responsible for empirical patterns. Candidates for knowledge are creative conceptions of objects existing within their contexts and contributing to environing effects. What is real is what can make a difference to something else, and what is knowably real marks that detectible difference for thinkers suspecting its role. Thinking's ability to craft and re-craft concepts for recasting ongoing engagements with reality is a theory of mentality offered by *pragmatism*.

Knowledge's goal of objectivity about the world can be reconciled with mind's knowing activity within the world. Minds are not just working with ideas after the world makes its impact. How the world affects knowers is itself controllable by intellects seeking genuine information. Whatever things are doing all by themselves has no value for knowledge. The meaning of objectivity cannot be "that answer that no one could ever find out," but instead "the answer that striving learners can discover." Every philosophy should at least agree that what is objective is something that thought can conform with. The alternative, taking objectivity to be what thought needn't conform to, leaves thought to wander lost in subjectivity.

Pragmatism, among all philosophies, takes most seriously the tenet that anything real is something to which thought may conform and confirm. A conception of something to be considered without any attendant consequences in the encounterable world is a conception of something not real. Conversely, only through conceiving possible empirical effects of a thing could there be a conception of that thing's reality. This is the heart of the pragmatic maxim.

In a later article, "What Pragmatism Is" from 1906, Peirce restated his central thesis.

> [A] conception, that is, the rational purport of a
> word or other expression, lies exclusively in its

conceivable bearing upon the conduct of life; so that, since obviously nothing that might not result from experiment can have any direct bearing upon conduct, if one can define accurately all the conceivable experimental phenomena which the affirmation or denial of a concept could imply, one will have therein a complete definition of the concept, and there is absolutely nothing more in it. For this doctrine he [Peirce] invented the name pragmatism.[9]

Something in utter isolation cannot be conceived as having any properties, capacities, powers (and the like), and hence it cannot have any explanatory role with regard to anything else. Unless there are empirical consequences from a thing's reality, confirmations and disconfirmations are not possible, and no truths about that thing, including its existence, could be asserted.

Knowledge on Trial

Pragmatism does not reduce a thing's reality to just its discernible effects, nor does it collapse the distinction between truth and reality. Pragmatism is a robust realism.

Pragmatism does identify the truth of a thing's actuality with the confirmation of that thing's capacity to yield specific discernible effects in the world. For pragmatism, a real thing undergoes its own variations in order to effect change for anything else. Something actively real must be potentially *realizable*, in the double sense of becoming *manifest* for the world through its effects, as well as becoming *evident* for the inquirer through observations of those effects. The truth lies neither in what is evident nor in what is real, but rather in the coordination of what a real thing can perform with what the inquiring knower can confirm.

Truth, in short, must make a difference, because things being real do make a difference. In 1907 James stated his version of the pragmatic maxim in *Pragmatism*:

> But the great assumption of the intellectualists is that truth means essentially an inert static relation. When you've got your true idea of anything, there's an end of the matter. You're in possession; you *know*; you have fulfilled your thinking destiny . . . Pragmatism, on the other hand, asks its usual question. "Grant an idea or belief to be true," it says, "what concrete difference will its being true make in anyone's actual life? How will the truth be realized? What experiences will be different from those which would obtain if the belief were false? What, in short, is the truth's cash-value in experiential terms?"[10]

Truth, in short, must make a difference, because things being real do make a difference.

Intellectualism (rationalism) is satisfied with unrealizable truth, matched with invariant reality on one side and paired to static mentality on the other. Truth in itself is beyond a knower's appreciation; only an idea or belief gets realized by a knower, which may or may not happen to be true (that depends on reality, not any knower), so that a knower could possess a true belief without realizing its truth.

Rationalism does not fail to emphasize how a knower can appreciate true beliefs through intellectual justification. However, a well-justified belief is not automatically true, according to rationalism, since the rationalist definition of truth is not simply "justified belief" but something rather like "justified true belief." Truth must be a third required factor for knowledge, since the truth of a belief depends solely on what reality is like, not what a knower has been able to justify.

As sensible as this triadic approach may seem, it is impossible for a knower to participate in the making of a truth, for this rationalist view of truth. Knowledge is attained only if its three terms—reality, truth, and belief—remain in rigid alignment. If a knower modifies a belief after further thoughtful justification, that belief may no longer be true.

For rationalism, a knower cannot change a truth. A knower can change a belief, but changing a truth requires altering a reality, and knowers must never alter the reality to be known. The objective of knowledge is independent reality, not dependent matters. Creating an object and thereby making an appreciable "truth" is no proper method for authentic knowledge. Knowledge is about what truly is, not about what knowers are doing; what knowers are doing is constantly changing, while realities to be known are statically indifferent to knowers. If knowers would know reality as it truly is, they must cease all interference with realities.

Strictures against the knower's interference with realities are upheld by every modern type of rationalism, from objective idealism and scientific materialism to positivistic empiricism.

For objective idealism, what is already known by absolute mind can at best be partially reduplicated within a knower's own mind. For a materialism or physicalism, science controls experimental conditions only in order to reveal what was already naturally there. As for positivism, the point of perception is to directly appreciate what is presently given to the senses, not to infuse perceptions with the knower's prior conceptions.

With each of these three options, the relationship between a knower's mentality and the reality to be known is contorted into a conundrum.

For idealism, the knower's mind is trying to duplicate the schematically perfect knowledge. Since this imperfect finite mind is already contained within the absolute mind, that condition of knowledge duplication could never be confirmed by any knower. For physicalism, since the theorizer's hypothesis only concerns what something real is already doing, the schema for legitimate experiments must never elicit alterations to that postulated reality. That seems sound in principle, yet the satisfaction of this condition is not itself confirmable by science. For positivism, the knower's perceptual beliefs should at most schematically reflect given perceptions as they are, not in a distorted manner introduced by thought. Conceptual relations inherent to a perceptual belief must be due only to an intrinsically non-conceptual perception, by way of some unknowable relation between them. Idealism, physicalism, and positivism are each missing a crucial link.

Other versions of rationalism invariably reach that same skeptical dead-end. Rationalism effectively forbids a knower's knowledge that truth conditions are truly satisfied. The truth-relation is foremost set by a reality independent from the knower's mentality, while the rationalistic promise that a mental schema rightly aligns a knower's beliefs with reality is not confirmable by knowers. Knowers are left only with formal schemas and the mere hope, unprovable by any further philosophizing, that the shape of truths formed from that schema may match the shape of realities.

Kantian philosophy, and most of post-Kantian philosophy, including analytic philosophy and much continental philosophy, exemplified this inevitably skeptical conundrum. Pragmatist interpretations of Hegel[11] along with (enactivist) cognitive science, realistic phenomenology, and some philosophies of impermanence can avoid that dead-end, along with pragmatism itself.

Pragmatism's full resolution is the starkest of all alternatives: truthful knowledge creatively emerges from thoughtfully deliberate entanglements with continually changing realities. This alternative violates strictures of invariance set by rationalism, starting from (a) knowable reality is aloof from the activity of knowing; (b) truths about fundamental realities cannot vary across knowers or change over time; and (c) knowable truth cannot basically depend on the dynamic creativity of knowers.

Pragmatism firmly insists that the coordinating relationship of truth between knowing and reality must be brought into existence by reality-modifying engagements with the world. Rationalism always complains that workable ideas could, at best, luckily match up with stable realities. "What is useless may still be true, and what is useful may yet be false!" was the rationalist critique from all sides. No matter how empirically satisfying an idea could be, and worthy of the label of knowledge, the rationalist at most admits that this idea had to have been really true all along, long before that idea was confirmed or even confirmable.

It is precisely that "retrospective" view of truth from rationalism which pragmatism attempts to replace. John

Dewey's 1907 article "Reality and the Criterion for the Truth of Ideas" states the pragmatist view of truth in this way:

> After an idea is made true, we naturally say, in retrospect, "it was true all the time." Now this truism is quite innocuous as a truism, being just a restatement of the fact that the idea has, as matter of fact, worked successfully. But it may be regarded not as a truism but as furnishing some additional knowledge, as if it were, indeed, the dawning of a revelation regarding truth. Then it is said that the idea worked or was verified because it was already inherently, just as idea, the truth, the pragmatist, so it is said, making the error of supposing that it is true because it works. If one remembers that what the experimentalist means is that the effective working of an idea and its truth are one and the same thing—this working being neither the cause nor the evidence of truth but its nature—it is hard to see the point of this statement.[12]

With this bold statement about the irrelevance of "truth" prior to the effort to acquire knowledge, we can summarize pragmatist contentions about knowing and truth made by Peirce, James, and Dewey.

Summary

Conceptions of realities having any meaning for constructive explorations and rational inquiries must include real linkages with empirical matters. In order for a conception of something real to serve in inquiry's effort to develop the coordination leading to knowledge, that conception should include ideas of what may empirically follow from affirming it and denying it.

Imagination plays a crucial yet constrained role here for inquiry. Creative ideas need not have existential import to be meaningful, but if they are taken to be about something real, they must be developed into rational conceptions ready for application in worldly engagements and empirical inquiries.

For the pragmatist prospective view of truth, truths become true, and not merely known, through the engaging inquiries of knowers. Knowledge is pragmatically (experientially, empirically, experimentally) justified belief, and "truths" are simply alternative labels for beliefs known.

In short, "P is true" means "P is known," or perhaps "P is knowable" when a new truth is proposed. There is no further intellectual content to an assertion of truth beyond these meanings. "P is true" cannot just mean "P" because "P" by itself is either an assertion that P is known (on pragmatist terms), or it lacks a context needed to intend anything.

BEING AND THINKING

For pragmatism, truths accrue to successful engagements with the cooperative world, which is to say that knowable realities emerge through practical experiments to control outcomes.

A. Realities participate in knowledge-creation through productive activities of inquiring animals pursuing goals.

B. Results indicate how intelligent animals are discovering reliable procedures that elicit reacting realities.

Pragmatism takes scenarios A and B to be equivalent descriptions of one process: A and B are convertible and exchangeable without loss or distortion of meaning. Only connotations of words and preconceptions about terms would allow A and B to be read as different matters.

Grammatically, A and B suggest a directionality, from realities to inquiries to ends, or the reverse. Proposition A may sound more realistic and "objective" than B, if B seems "subjective" or even idealistic. A linguistic bias of selective emphasis could be at work as well. Proposition A allows for an emphasis on knowledge's confirmation of truth while B suggests an emphasis on mind's journey of discovery. All the same, pragmatism observes one and the same endeavor. Rival philosophies, especially philosophies of permanence, are compelled to disagree.

Thinking with Reality

To survey the philosophical landscape, five main features stand out. Pragmatism asserts that these five matters are bonded together, each in cohesion with the rest:

World—Truth—Mind—Purpose—Value

Non-pragmatist philosophies tear away a trio for metaphysical superiority while denigrating the rest. Rationalism orients Mind to Truth–World. Subjectivism centers Value in Mind–Purpose. Absolutism identifies Mind with World–Value. Pragmatism's commitment to all of them in concert is a fourth main option, while the abandonment of all five characterizes the fifth option of Mysticism.

Let rationalism have its say first, castigating pragmatism for tying knowledge down to variable practicalities. Where does the elimination of value from knowledge and truth leave mind? An intellect aiming at truth is best insulated from affective and emotional biases, to stay impersonally objective. Practicalities divert our particular minds; intellectualities unify mind. Mentality is thus divided internally, either facing reality or entertaining fancies. The intellect has a primary purpose, to seek truth for its own sake. Pragmatism, according to rationalism, allows other goals to steer knowledge. As the rationalist view of pragmatism says, "knowledge is valuable, so what is valuable is known," to put pragmatism into a fallacious slogan. Truth is most valuable, among many values, but nothing pragmatic follows, as far as rationalism can see.

What really gives a proposition its truth value? Rationalism counters with its own slogan, "truth's value cannot imply value's truth." Since most any thought could be valued at some time by someone somewhere, too many ideas are valuable and hence knowable as true. That vast cacophony of truths would never be internally consistent— endless contradictions ensue, where instances of "P" and "not-P," cases of "S is P" and "S is not P," and beliefs about "R exists" and "R does not exist" are allowable as simultaneously true.

Suspending the rule of non-contradiction (and the law of excluded middle) opens up the wide vista of complete relativism where very little has to be wrong. Robust truth, for rationalism, preserves non-contradiction and prevents relativism. Regulated by robust truth, known ideas are about what objectively exists (not whatever desire objectifies). Robust truth therefore filters out divisive Purpose and distractive Value from the intellectual mind seeking unified reality rather than chaotic practicality. That unity to an objective reality has the form of that singular proposition of stable fact, where fact-shaped realities give propositions their truth values. What is factual can be knowable, as rationality corresponds with Truth–World.[1]

The next voice to speak up on behalf of knowledge is subjectivism, which is no more impressed by truth correspondence than pragmatism, but it discards unitary and fixed truth altogether. Avoiding relativism at all costs mustn't demand too high a price, for a mind trying to know "the" truth. Subjectivism is compelled to ask, "how could it be claimed with surety that 'minds are many, but truth is one'?"

Tearing mentality apart to liberate disinterested knowing sets up the "intellect" over and against the rest of vital thinking. In the process, nothing guarantees that an intellect truly attains knowledge. That independence of reality from mentality instead opens a gap between a proposition beheld by a mind and a fact beholden to reality. Formulating a proposition with needed precision would always be a matter of luck. (And stepping outside of all mentality to inspect realities before assembling propositions isn't humanly possible.) Any actual fit bridging that gap cannot itself be an intelligible object of thought for any subject.

The thought that "the proposition P* that 'there a fact F corresponding with proposition P' matches fact F* about the mind–reality relationship" is a sort of mental stuttering, or an eliminable recursion. In other words, to assert "P is really true" is not different from a person just asserting P. All the same, assertions are assertions made in a person's mind, not truths revealed to minds. The logical dualism between the aloof intellect and the practical mind, and the ontological dualism separating thoughts from things, deflates confidence that any intellect is actually knowing truths about things, rather than just relations among ideas. For subjectivism, correspondence is a bridge to nowhere.

These are all complaints heard from pragmatists too. Rationalism decidedly risks skepticism, ensuring that the intellect avoids relativism but leaving minds minding only their own thoughts. Under such circumstances, subjectivism concludes that thoughtful minds are at least known best. Skepticism about knowing external truths still leaves plenty for minds to think about pursuing. World and Truth can therefore be dropped from consideration.

With World and Truth sidelined, Subjectivism points out that a mind surely knows what it wants and knows how to think in ways conducive to attaining those ends. The nature of the subject lies in willing, not reasoning. Thinking should be guided by attentive Purpose and attractive Value. If this stance is a kind of relativism, with each subjective mind determining for itself what serves as veritable belief, at least skepticism is no longer a worry. Let knowing be determinable through each mind's own pursuits. What is desirable can be knowable, by the plurality of Mind–Purpose.[2]

Skepticism towards truth marks the key pivot for absolutism as well. Both rationalism and subjectivism, one reluctantly and the other eagerly, raise skepticism about truth. However, such skepticism is no wiser for its admission of universal misconception and error, since truth need not be lost. To class all thinking as erroneous presupposes the possibility of correct thinking. It is not possible to "miss" in one's "take" about some matter without the potential, however slight, for a veritable "hit." Throw one's hand up into the night sky to vaguely point in the direction of the overhead stars—no bystander would comment, "That's a poor way to point at Vega."

Where no "fit" for a thought is in place, no possible "fact" of accuracy or inaccuracy is around. Likewise, for absolutism, the fact of inaccuracy implies a possible fit for a thought is around. Assigning wrongness anywhere lies within the same cognition as admitting rightness some-where. Therefore, non-contradiction prevails over any thinking more rational than insanity (thus refuting relativism and subjectivism). There is no error without truth, and not merely in the abstract but also for concrete truth in the actual world where errors are plentiful.

Any mind's thinking with purport about some matter, thereby classifiable as accurate or inaccurate, demonstrates the inherent value of veracity to mentality. Absolutism, better than subjectivism, captures the essence of mind. Thinking cannot be completely unrealistic; the purposive activity of mentality presumes an objective reality as knowable, since veracity cannot be conceived as inherently unknowable. Setting out from skepticism ends with admitting that knowledge is realistic, and that reality must be truly knowable by mentality. Not the mentality of particular minds in their erroneous partiality and plurality, to be sure, but rather the absolute (non-relative and unitary) Minded Reality.

For absolutism, individual minds are themselves incomplete and insufficient, and less real than the single reality they intend. Valuable verity dispels relativism and implies objectivity, requiring the universal structuring of what would otherwise be chaos. Transcending fragmentary subjectivity and incomplete purpose arrives at the whole finality of Value, the full attainment of all purposes, where any distinction between true mind and true reality vanishes. What is real is already knowable, within the absolute totality of World–Value.[3]

The worldviews of Truth–World (rationalism), Mind–Purpose (subjectivism), and World–Value (absolutism) do not exhaust philosophical options. Besides many impoverished philosophies trying to blend incongruent samplings from the set [world, truth, mind, purpose, value], there are two other major options: Mysticism and Pragmatism.

Mysticism proposes a reconciliation among [world, truth, mind, purpose, value] by denying a key tenet to each rival worldview. Against Purpose–Mind, it rejects the view that mind's willing attention yields what is known, because no effort is needed to be mindful of what truly needs minding. Against Truth–Reality, it denies the principle that what is knowable must be conceptual and propositional. The law of non-contradiction is thus irrelevant (so the objective–subjective dichotomy dissolves).

Against World–Value, mysticism doubts that true worth depends on conformity with deliberate structure. No conceptual work is called for where immediacy shines forth in purity. Letting go of those three tenets permits mentality itself to slow and find rest in the peace of unconcern, non-affirmation, and non-duality. Non-willing inattention allows undifferentiated oneness of indefinite and unlimited emptiness, while individuality becomes non-consequential as distinctive activity gradually blends unresistingly into unitary harmony. If there yet be verity, let it be called "Illumination" in the placid unity of authenticity–awareness–attentiveness, as focus stays in the present, the fully worthy mode of reality.

Pragmatism has little in common with mysticism as a worldview, although an ideal of verity in experiential harmony comports with pragmatism's view of knowledge.[4]

Being and Thinking

The option of pragmatism reconciles all five [world, truth, mind, purpose, value] by affirming, with adjustments, key tenets of the other worldviews: mind's purposiveness, knowledge's objectivity, the world's worth, and verity's harmony. Specifically, consider these modified tenets: (a) mind's deliberate attentiveness experimentally yields what is learnable; (b) knowledge requires the work of conceptual and propositional refinement; and (c) worth's acquisition increases from conformity with practical structure.

These adjusted tenets display a dynamic dimension, transmuting the set [world, truth, mind, purpose, value] into [reality, veracity, mentality, activity, finality]. Furthermore, to ensure that no logical or ontological gap opens, this worldview additionally affirms that (d) intelligent minds actively operate as practical structurings; (e) knowing veritably grows from experimental trials of conceptual/propositional refinements; and (f) practical realities are the final goals of any knowledge worth acquiring. Finally, knowing arises from harmony, that holistic harmony among the five:

Reality, Verity, Mentality, Activity, Finality

In this philosophical harmonization, each intrinsically depends on the rest, and their attachment is indistinguishable from the entrainment of:

Ends, Deeds, Thoughts, Knowns, Reals

Pragmatism's rivals cannot fully explain knowledge, and risk abandoning knowledge entirely. Pragmatism can agree with rationalism that robust truth serves as a regulative ideal guiding knowledge towards objectivity. Rationalism's insistence that realities are preformed for knowledge's conformity compels pragmatism to object to the resulting dualities responsible for skepticism. With rationalism, if minds happen to entertain knowledge, they couldn't realize it, subverting the point of rationalism's adherence to permanence.

Subjectivism, like pragmatism, regards dualism and skepticism as poor rewards for protecting truth from relativism. Some types of subjectivism join philosophies of impermanence (found among personalisms and existentialisms for example), but their efforts to rebuild some degree of objectivity to avoid solipsism bring them towards pragmatism. Pragmatism similarly regards mentality as wholly organized around purpose, but it expects a plurality of minds to organize in pursuit of knowledgeable endeavors. Truth isn't abandoned for relativism, because workable beliefs tend to converge in objective agreement among cooperative inquiring minds.

Pragmatism agrees with absolutism that thinking with purport does presuppose engagements with realities able to comport (or not) with mentality. However, like rationalism, absolutism assumes the availability of precise conceptions, exact enough to fit concept-shaped realities. If individual minds can correctly conceive some realities, those minds can't be deemed less real than the reality they know; if individual minds cannot correctly conceive realities, those minds never apprehend the Absolute Mind, and skepticism returns.

On rationalism, subjectivism, absolutism, and even mysticism, individual minds are ultimately left where they began, with their thoughtful pursuits of valuable ends attainable only by intelligently engaging the world. Truth is there, and nowhere else. Philosophies of permanence refuse to see truth's natural home and habitat with the mentalities creating it. "The truth is out there," in the great beyond, outside the warm embrace of experience and life. In modern European philosophy, that principle was embodied in Immanuel Kant's tenet that a "Ding an sich" ("thing-in-itself") that never appears is somehow responsible for delivering fresh perceptual content for the mind's digestion.

Peirce, James, and Dewey regarded pragmatism as the eventual destination for philosophy's repudiation of Kant's thing-in-itself in any form. Peirce recollected how his pragmatism of the 1870s, which he later called "pragmaticism," eliminated that Kantian feature.

> The present writer was a pure Kantist until he was forced by successive steps into Pragmaticism. The Kantist has only to abjure from the bottom of his heart the proposition that a thing-in-itself can, however indirectly, be conceived; and then correct the details of Kant's doctrine accordingly ... [5]

To "correct the details," in Peirce's understated phrasing, a large-scale reconstruction of modern philosophy would be required, as James and Dewey fully realized as well. By 1890 Dewey was pointing out how a philosophy lacking a thing-in-itself could not isolate thought from reality.

> For if we reconstruct the Kantian theory of knowledge upon its own basis and method of analysis, doing away with the thing-in-itself, the result is to show that the merely logical, equally with the merely ontological, is an impossible abstraction.

The merely logical is not at all; the logical is only as the thought-factor in the entire determination of experience . . .[6]

In that same year of 1890, James published his path-breaking *The Principles of Psychology*, in which he replaced the Kantian dualism between relational thought and un-related things with the experiential field of related things inviting thought's explorations.[7]

In a 1904 article, "Humanism and Truth," James defended pragmatism under the "humanism" label by declaring that thought seeks truth in the prevailing relations among things in experience.

There may or may not be an extra-experiential 'ding an sich' that keeps the ball rolling, or an 'absolute' that lies eternally behind all the successive determinations which human thought has made. But within our experience itself at any rate, humanism says, some determinations show themselves as being independent of others; some questions, if we ever ask them, can only be answered in one way; some beings, if we ever suppose them, must be supposed to have existed previously to the supposing; some relations, if they exist ever, must exist as long as their terms exist. Truth thus means, according to humanism, the relation of less fixed parts of experience (predicates) to other relatively more fixed parts (subjects); and we are not required to seek it in a relation of experience as such to anything beyond itself.[8]

When philosophy stops trying to conceive the strictly inconceivable, such as that "thing-in-itself," then it is no longer tempted to postulate as real anything so isolated from all conceptual and mental relationality. Metaphysical realism justifies a thorough repudiation of all idealisms by denying that "the real" needs to have any relation to thought. However, to realistically explain how thought has something real as its object, some relation between them (besides sheer accidental coincidence, which is just the absence of explanation) is still required. Avoiding that requirement yields the mysterious thing-in-itself.

The pragmatists situated cognition and its transformative work within the broader context of experience. Reality can neither be entirely cognitive, nor extra-cognitive, but reality must in principle be conceivable in relation to what is experiential. In general, it is impossible to separate what only "thought" is, entirely apart from what "reality" is. Only by surrendering the temptation to dualistically divorce thoughts from things can philosophy achieve any objectivity.

Like James, Dewey regarded thought as actively engaging with the relations among the multiplicity of matters in

Only by surrendering
the temptation to
dualistically divorce
thoughts from things
can philosophy achieve
any objectivity.

the world, rather than imposing relations among disaggregate entities unable to compose a world.

> The inherent difficulty of the Kantian philosophy—that of showing how two absolutely antithetical elements coming from two opposite sources, one from the thing-in-itself, the other from thought—led his successors to move in the direction of the concept of an "absolute experience," an experience so comprehensive and permanent as to cancel the Kantian dualism.
>
> Meanwhile other developments, partly within philosophy and partly within the biological and social sciences, were making for a radically different conception of experience . . . The main features of the resulting concept of experience may be associated with the two chief connotations of the popular, non-technical use of the term: namely, (a) to try a thing out, to test in action, and (b) to undergo, to endure, to suffer. With the first, or more active sense, experiment and the deliberate control of experience are connected; with the second, or more passive sense, the dependence of the individual upon contact with a world, social and natural, beyond himself . . . But in both cases there is some outreaching effort to modify the environment in the interests of life.[9]

For these pragmatists, mentality and objectivity naturally go together, because what is never thought is unreal and what is only thought is subjective.

The stern lesson learned from Kant's dichotomies is that a philosophical effort to subtract away all relations to mentality and thought in order to consider what may remain, in its unthought and non-conceived purity, is a pointless quest, forever unable to discern what that remainder is "really" like, or what mental thought "adds" to it.

There is nothing about experience insulated from thought or awaiting the first touch of thought, and there is nothing beyond experience forever unrelated to possible thought. We think that something surprisingly encountered has not yet been recognized because thought's attention promptly provokes further cognition of it; we think that something outside of experience is causing an encountered event because thought's conception preemptively evokes further relations with it. We intelligibly suppose that unknown matters still await our cognition by conceiving how those matters might be directly or indirectly encounterable. The dark side of the Moon was objectively discoverable by thought (not subjectively created in thought) due to cognition's capacity to guide activities towards encounters with it. By contrast, what is entirely unthought must be left inconceivable and ignored by philosophy and science, which seek realities.

Since the unthought beyond experience is indistinguishable from the unreal, the real must be conceived as relatable to thought within experience. What is objective cannot be unreal, so objectivity lies in the real's relations for the experienceable. "Experience" for pragmatism is hardly subjective, since it is nothing other than the world encounterable in activity, which is what remains intact for philosophy after the static "thing-in-itself" and the rigid "thought-in-itself" are both eliminated from consideration.

Thinking and Objectivity

Pragmatism rests on experience, but not on a misconception of experience imposed by rationalism's demand that reasoning proceeds in some cognitive realm beyond experiencing. Despite empiricism's resistance against rationalism during the course of modern philosophy, full trust in actual lived experience, beyond the traps of subjectivism and idealism, was left for pragmatism's revolution.[10]

Dewey's comparison of the old and new empiricism drew attention to inference's proper place within proactive experience.

> (i) In the orthodox view, experience is regarded primarily as a knowledge-affair. But to eyes not looking through ancient spectacles, it assuredly

appears as an affair of the intercourse of a living being with its physical and social environment. (ii) According to tradition experience is (at least primarily) a psychical thing, infected throughout by "subjectivity." What experience suggests about itself is a genuinely objective world which enters into the actions and sufferings of men and undergoes modifications through their responses. (iii) So far as anything beyond a bare present is recognized by the established doctrine, the past exclusively counts. Registration of what has taken place, reference to precedent, is believed to be the essence of experience. Empiricism is conceived of as tied up to what has been, or is, "given." But experience in its vital form is experimental, an effort to change the given; it is characterized by projection, by reaching forward into the unknown; connexion with a future is its salient trait. (iv) The empirical tradition is committed to particularism. Connexions and continuities are supposed to be foreign to experience, to be by-products of dubious validity. An experience that is an undergoing of an environment and a striving for its control in new directions is pregnant with connexions. (v) In the traditional notion experience and thought are antithetical terms. Inference, so far as it is other than a revival of what has been given in the past, goes beyond experience; hence it is either invalid, or else a measure of desperation by which, using experience as a springboard, we jump out to a world of stable things and other selves. But experience, taken free of the restrictions imposed by the older concept, is full of inference. There is, apparently, no conscious experience without inference; reflection is native and constant.[11]

Experiencing the world is far more a matter of what is taken, not given. An interesting thing in the world and an interested observer together yield valuable meanings and valid understandings; neither side by itself yields much of cognitive merit. This is the view on active experience that Dewey labelled as "transactional" and grounds all experimentation. The objectivity that empiricism promises is attained with pragmatism's insistence that thought performs its work out in the world, not within consciousness.

That "thing-in-itself" can assume many guises in philosophies of permanence, both realistic and idealistic, as they insist that objectivity rests on realities kept apart from the flux and flex of experience. Likewise, that "thought-in-itself" lingers for rationalist philosophies as they demand that the right kind of thought needed for relating to realities must be knowable in itself. Abandoning these mythical creatures liberates thought to rejoin the world.

As far as pragmatism can see, a fixation on necessity turns away from objectivity. For example, "analytic" judgments allegedly display necessity, contingent on a mental act sustaining two ideas jointly in thought. Another person's mental comparison of those ideas may find no such necessity, leaving necessity a matter of subjectivity. Complaining that any dissenter "doesn't know the meaning of those ideas" begs the question, since "the meaning" here concerns the necessity to be demonstrated, not assumed. "But I can't conceive otherwise" is similarly a statement about one's subjective thinking and nothing more.

Asserting that rational thinkers already know "the meaning" of an idea makes a claim about another thought-in-itself transcending actual thinkers. Language helps to create this mirage. Speakers of a shared language know the meanings of its terms, so any necessity to conceivability is relative to linguistic competency. In general, conceptual necessity is bound to subjectivity and relativism, not any sort of universal objectivity.

Pragmatism is content with linguistic relativism for stable public meanings, provided that linguistic communities acknowledge their responsibility for altering and inventing meanings of conceptions to keep up with enlarging experience and the growth of knowledge. Scientific communities establish and adjust the meanings of their terminologies at a rapid pace, but linguistic drift and development also characterizes the slower pace of entire societies.

Rationalists still asserting that there remain "true concepts" to guarantee necessities, above and beyond all linguistic communities, are seeking that thought-in-itself as thinkable by Mind, not just actual minds, so rationalism leads to absolute idealism. What does such a Mind think about? The thought-in-itself returns back to the thing-in-itself, which is to say, nonentity.

Let a proposition be deemed assertible with necessity because nothing conceivable negates it. When nothing conceivable could falsify a proposition, it is compatible with anything. Yet a proposition compatible with any-thing refers to nothing, on Peirce's conception principle. Hence, a necessary proposition cannot refer to anything.

In consequence, the kinds of objective propositions about the world that are conceived as practically necessary cannot be analytic. The formula F=MA (force equals mass times acceleration) involves three concepts, each complex enough to defy a simultaneous intuition of them exposing how each is "contained" in the others. Pragmatism finds a use for formulas within empirical knowledge, and to that extent they can participate in objectivity.

Pragmatism's avoidance of the thought-in-itself per-mits it to transform the analytic–synthetic categoriza-tion into a distinction between "formulaic" and "concretic" propositions. A formulaic proposition binds concepts so that applying one in a practical situation prescribes that applicability of the others. A concretic proposition predicts discernible effects from an encounter with something. "Combustion is the exothermic chemical reaction of fast oxidization" is a formulaic proposition. "Burning a kilogram of propane yields 11,950 kilocalories" is a concretic proposition.[12]

Both formulaic and concretic propositions are empirical: they are learned empirically, their meanings are exclusively empirical in import, and they are vulnerable to replacement by improved knowledge. Both express highly credible items of knowledge, but concretic knowledge justifies formulaic knowledge, never the reverse. The discovery of concretic truths inspire the conception of formulaic truths, and that assemblage of concretic truths justifies the further application of formulaic truths in fresh experimental inquiries to make further concrete discoveries.

Formulaic propositions play the role of premised knowledge within the methodologies of inquiries, with a status "prior" to the opening of specific empirical investigations, but there is nothing "a priori" about them in any Kantian sense. They are not universally necessary, they had no truth status before experiential learning, and they are disconfirmable in the long run. Again, linguistic competence within a knowledge community arouses a mirage of necessity immune from ongoing empirical matters.

That mirage of formulaic immunity is all a matter of practical convenience in the short run, when it is impossible to inquire into everything. Pragmatism understands how, during any empirical inquiry, some matters are regarded as secure stabilities while others are questionable variabilities. Paradigm shifts happening within one's own lifetime allow one to witness how eternal verity can get discarded as useless verbiage.

Summary

Pragmatism surpasses and replaces the dichotomy that truth is either about the outer world of things or about the inner world of ideas. The active engagement occurring between what we are observing and how we are thinking is responsible for our judgments about whatever we are dealing with. The "objectivist" and "subjectivist" stances are unified by pragmatism's "transactional" alternative.

As the next chapter explains, pragmatism's resolute avoidance of both the thing-in-itself and the thought-in-itself permits it to surmount epistemological puzzles over the relationship between the knower and the known, such as ancient philosophy's Problem of the Criterion and modern philosophy's Gettier Problem.

PRAGMATISM VERSUS EPISTEMOLOGY

Pragmatism is the sensible alternative to metaphysical inflations for "truth" into matters knowable as certainties, rigid patterns of inference reducing methodology to rationalism, or static facts pertaining to a mysterious reality beyond thought. Pragmatism neither abandons realism nor collapses into relativism, and it permits more flexible understandings about the role of truth in knowledge.

Some pragmatists have preferred to label as "truth" just those bodies of knowledge already highly warranted from past inquiries. Others prefer to view "truth" within methodological justifications as they occur during ongoing inquiries. Still others reserve "truth" to point to the potential for improved knowledge through future inquiries.

Distinguishing practical conceptions of truth is a longstanding feature of pragmatism, and pragmatists have found value in all three mentioned here.[1] A concept of truth as an honorific label bestowed on acquired knowledge is compatible with another concept of truth as a regulative ideal for reliable methodology, and both comport well with conceiving truth as an idealization about unlimited inquiry. They abandon rationalism's criterion of reality–independence for knowledge.

Objective Knowledge

Charles Peirce, William James, and John Dewey regarded their approaches to understanding inquiry, knowledge, and truth as rivals and replacements for dominant Western views about the nature of knowledge. Each pragmatist noted sharp disagreements with epistemological stances, particularly those indebted to, and descended from, tenets about knowledge and reality which they took to be affirmations of Socrates and Plato. The overthrow of rationalistic epistemology itself was promised. What precisely are the essential issues about knowledge and truth that pragmatism must dispute?

In *The Quest for Certainty*, Dewey discerns interlocking tenets about knowledge and reality in Plato, Aristotle, and much of Greek thought. "The first and foremost is that there is complete correspondence between knowledge in its true meaning and what is real. What is known, what is true for cognition, is what is real in being." This tenet is grounded, Dewey explains, in another tenet that "only the completely fixed and unchanging can be real." He continues: "Secondly, the theory of knowledge has its basic premises fixed by the same doctrine. For knowledge to be certain must relate to that which has antecedent existence or essential being."[2]

This theory of knowledge effectively demands that

... what is known is antecedent to the mental act of observation and inquiry, and is totally unaffected by these acts, otherwise it would not be fixed and unchangeable. This negative condition, that the processes of search, investigation, reflection, involved in knowledge relate to something having prior being, fixes once for all the main characters attributed to mind, and to the organs of knowing. They must be outside what is known, so as not to interact in any way with the object to be known.[3]

The requirement that the act of knowing cannot possibly alter the object of knowledge was therefore an objective for knowledge, and that peculiar act of knowing then became an item for epistemic interest in its own right.

So long as a knower cannot ensure the proper aloofness of knowing from the known, that knower cannot fully justify a claim to knowledge. The knowing relation therefore emerged as a matter of curiosity, and then concern, and finally as a matter itself requiring verification.

In short, the putative knowing relation itself became a candidate for knowledge—indeed, it became a crucial criterion for knowledge. It is one thing to ask, "What is knowledge?" and another to ask, "What can be known about the knowing relation?" Furthermore, a knowing relation between the knower and the known leaves three matters for investigation: the known's reality outside of a knowing relation, the knower within a knowing relation, and the nature of the relation between knowing and the known.

Dewey observed in *The Quest for Certainty* how modern philosophy perpetuated this view of knowledge as a concern for the peculiar relationship between mind and reality. Must the knowing relation be known by a relating knower to be about the known as it is unrelated to being known? He derided this theory of knowledge as a mere "spectator theory," akin to a naïve theory of vision.

Philosophy can't be so naïve, Dewey urged. The knowing relation required by this theory of knowledge would be akin to an observer only able to detect an object by shining a light upon it, all the while trying to know what the real object as it is unlit would truly be like. Dewey went back to ancient Greek thought, and especially Plato, to fault its fascination with a second immaterial kind of thought able to illuminate things as they truly are. This fascination, according to Dewey, arose from mathematics.

Mathematical conceptions as expressions of pure thought have also seemed to provide the open gateway to a realm of essence that is independent of existence, physical or mental—a self-subsisting realm of ideal and eternal objects which are the objects of the highest—that is, the most assured—knowledge. As was earlier noted, the Euclidean geometry was undoubtedly the pattern for the development of a formally rational logic; it was also a marked factor in leading Plato to his doctrine of a world of supersensible and superphysical ideal objects. The procedure of mathematics has, moreover, always been the chief reliance of those who have asserted that the demonstrated validity of all reflective thinking depends upon rational truths immediately known without any element of inference entering in. For mathematics was supposed to rest upon a basis of first truths or axioms, self-evident in nature, and needing only that the eye of reason should fall upon them to be recognized for what they are. The function of indemonstrables, of axioms and definitions, in mathematical deduction has been the ground for the distinction between intuitive and discursive reason, just as deductions have been taken to be the convincing proof that there is a realm of pure essences logically connected with one another:—

universals having internal bonds with one another.[4]

Dewey was a veteran of the great epistemology debates which had raged since the 1890s when he began formulating his pragmatism. He offered an empirical way to understand logic in practice after its liberation from intuitions due to mathematics.

William James knew those debates well. His titanic battle with his Harvard colleague, Josiah Royce, over knowledge and reality were played out before a generation of their students. Many of them went on to shape American philosophy's prioritization of mental philosophy and epistemology for the next fifty years.

The vice of epistemology, for James, was its intellectualism. Like Dewey, James faulted the Greek fascination with a permanent and aloof realm of being that attracts the exclusive aim of knowledge. Whatever is within a knower permitting that knowing relation, Greek philosophers typically inferred, must itself be rigid and unchanging too. James points behind Plato to the figure of Socrates, who sought to capture conceptual essences in verbal definitions. His 1910 work *A Pluralistic Universe* identifies the basic issue:

Intellectualism in the vicious sense began when Socrates and Plato taught that what a thing really is, is told us by its *definition*. Ever since Socrates we have been taught that reality consists of essences, not of appearances, and that the essences of things are known whenever we know their definitions. So first we identify the thing with a concept and then we identify the concept with a definition, and only then, inasmuch as the thing *is* whatever the definition expresses, are we sure of apprehending the real essence of it or the full truth about it.[5]

As for the founder of pragmatism, Charles Peirce, he never considered himself to be an epistemologist. Peirce held little regard for the term (it came into use in the 1850s) and less regard for self-styled epistemologists of his day.

Peirce's interpretation of the Greek use of "episteme" associated it with "comprehension": "It is the ability to define a thing in such a manner that all its properties shall be corollaries from its definition."[6] This statement, from the unpublished treatise *Minute Logic* (c.1902) in a section titled "A Detailed Classification of the Sciences," is accompanied by his view that "episteme" must never be translated as "science" and cannot be equated with what moderns call knowledge.

Does epistemology rest on an exaggerated role for the knowing relation and the essential definition? Pragmatism views traditional philosophy back to the Greeks as a "quest for certainty," as Dewey put it. Rationalism was the core of comprehending knowledge. Following views defended in Plato's dialogues, knowledge claims should use rigidly conceived terms so that no contradictions or counterexamples can be found. Knowing one's concepts with unimpeachable definitions must be prior to substantive claims about any matters.

After this rationalist stance is settled, certainty cannot be compromised. Demonstrable confidence in one's avoidance of error is necessary. The Greek tradition imbued the philosophical problem of knowledge with the worry that a person cannot know something to be true so long as its falsity remains a possibility. Furthermore, this Greek tradition also expected a criterial definition of knowledge to be indubitable as well.

These expectations about knowledge were inherited by modern epistemology. For any subject matter, whether a concept, a term, a definition, a description, and so on, knowledge is of what is true, not what is false. Knowledge, if it truly be knowing, cannot err.

Principle of "Inerrant Knowing": Unless it can be known that there are no possible ways where a person P will fail to truly know X, P cannot know X.

Pragmatism must dispute this epistemological claim. Due to this principle, traditional epistemology suffers from the two Roycean cases, the four types of Gettier problems, and the three paradoxes of the Criterion, explained next.

Knowing Knowledge

Epistemology requires the examination of each situation in which P is a candidate for knowing X, to make sure that a situation doesn't match any of these three situations:

Hypothetical Situation (a) imagines that P's method of ascribing D about X will require X to have F and possibly not-F.

Hypothetical Situation (b) imagines that there is some N that is a Y (but not an X) that can fit P's method of ascribing D about an X.

Hypothetical Situation (c) imagines that there is some M that is X that cannot fit P's method of ascribing D about an X.

Situation (a) imposes the rule that something cannot be ascribed contradictory features; situation (b) expects that no counterexample can be wrongly included with an ascription; situation (c) expects that no counterexample can be wrongly excluded from an ascription.

Furthermore, in accord with the "Inerrant Knowing" principle, unless P knows that P knows X, P cannot know X. Epistemology accordingly requires the further examination of each situation in which P is a candidate for knowing X, so that P cannot accidentally obtain knowledge. This means that:

P must know that the applied method ascribing D to X won't lead to contradictory attributions to X;

P must know that the applied method ascribing D to X won't lead P to affirm that a Y is D; and

P must know that the applied method ascribing D to X would reliably lead P to affirm D of each real X.

Therefore, three additional situations would prevent P from knowledge.

Hypothetical Situation (d) finds that P doesn't know that P's method of ascribing D to X might expect X to be F and not-F; so, P cannot know a real X is D.

Hypothetical Situation (e) finds that P doesn't know that P's method of ascribing D to X is reliably about a real X instead of some other Y; so, P cannot know that a real X is D.

Hypothetical Situation (f) finds that P doesn't know that P's method ascribing D to X is reliably leading P to affirm that each real X is D; so, P cannot know that a real X is D.

Hypothetical Situations (a) and (d) yield what can be called the Roycean Cases. Josiah Royce formulated his complaints against realism by arguing that realism prizes the real object's independence at the price of the object staying knowable.[7] In a similar fashion, John Dewey critiqued epistemology's reliance on the ubiquity of the knowledge relation. If there is a unique knowing relation between the knower and the known, it is impossible to confirm a successful operation of the knowing process.[8]

Both Royce and Dewey pointed out how there is no way to know if this ubiquitous knowing is occurring, so long as knowing is an external relation. The fact, if it is a fact, that a knower is in the knowing relation would not be automatically known as well, since it is not part of the knowledge. Knowledge would be a matter of luck, so far as anyone could tell, including the knower. And if knowing is instead an internal relation, then one can know when and what one knows, but how the known is known is in the relation to the knower, and it would not be known whether what is known also persists outside the knowing relation.

Situation (a), the first Roycean Case, is one in which a real entity X is supposed to agree to an ascription of D, while X is supposed to be D by itself. If X is D by itself, then X's possession of the Fs (the features/properties) included in D cannot depend in any way on anything that is not X. Those Fs are therefore intrinsic or essential to X; they involve relations internal to X, not external or accidental. But then D isn't a description of X—D is a (partial) definition of X. To merely define an X in the abstract does not amount to describing a real X; one can define plenty of nonexistent things. In order to describe X, P must include in D some external and accidental Fs for X to individuate and identify a real X. That arouses a serious risk that those Fs will contradict each other, and in any case, P's D will no longer describe X by itself. Consequently, P will fail to know a real X by itself.

Situation (d), the second Roycean Case, is one in which P tries to relationally know X as it is by itself (yes, that should sound problematic). How can P know that P's method of ascribing D to X is succeeding in knowing an X by itself? For P to know that X is exemplifying D for P, all of the Fs included in D have to be relational between X and P. Although P can know how X is exemplifying those Fs in relation to P, P cannot know if X possesses those Fs by itself when X isn't in an external relation with P. Therefore, P doesn't know whether P's method of ascribing D to X is expecting X to have Fs by itself and not have Fs by itself. Consequently, P cannot know that a real X is D.

Situations (b), (c), (e), and (f) yield so-called Gettier Cases.[9] As the epistemology literature after Gettier amply displays, many Gettier cases have been crafted to somehow show that instances of justified true belief are not actually knowledge. This section is only concerned with the four basic types of Gettier Cases which follow from "Inerrant Knowing." To describe these types, this taxonomy is used: Let N and M stand for individual nameable entities, while X and Y are generic things, and D is a description.

Situation (b) conceives of a specific N and a specific M, and X, in such a way that X fits D, this N is an X (fits D), M is not an X (doesn't fit D), M doesn't fit P's D of X, P reasonably applies D to M to discern an X, and P thereby affirms D of an X, so that P truly affirms an X fitting D. P truly affirms an X fitting D (since N is an X fitting D), but P knows that P's affirmation is only about M (which isn't truly an X). Common sense says that even though P reasonably and justifiably affirmed D of M and thereby affirmed a truth that "an X is D," P didn't affirm D of the genuine X that truly is D (that was N, not M). That's why common sense denies that P has knowledge of "an X is D."

Situation (c) conceives of a specific N and a specific M, and X, in such a way that P reasonably applies D to N at one moment and thereby truly affirms "X is D"; later, P again reasonably affirms "X is D" but N is absent and an identical M is now present, so P now thinks M is D while still affirming "X is D"; so there is some M that is X that doesn't fit P's method of ascribing D to X. That's why common sense denies that P has knowledge of "X is D."

Situation (e) conceives of a specific N, and X and Y, in such a way that P first affirms that N is D. N is truly Y, but P justifiably believes N is X instead, so P also affirms that X is D. "X is D" happens to be true, but P has no reasonable way to affirm that X is D. Although P affirms the truth "X is D," P doesn't know that the method ascribing D to X isn't reliable about a real X, so P doesn't know X is D.

Situation (f) conceives of a specific N, and X, in such a way that P ascribes D to N using a method not presently reliable, although P's method of ascribing D to Xs like N is ordinarily reliable. Despite the way that P's resulting ascription of D to N, and P's affirmation of "an X is D," happens to both be true, P doesn't presently know that P's method ascribing D to X is reliably leading to affirming that this real X (this N) is D; so P cannot know that a real X is D.

Many Gettier cases formulated in the expansive epistemological literature are specific versions of these four types.[10]

Paradoxes of Knowledge

If knowing that one knows applies to knowledge itself, the question must arise, Is a "Definition of Knowledge" itself knowable? The enterprise of "knowing knowledge" is launched.

Principle of "Knowing Knowledge": For P to have knowledge of real Knowledge, P must know an account of Knowledge that contains no contradictions and permits no counterexamples.

There are three types of conceivable situations where a person will fail to know real Knowledge:

1. Where P's account of knowledge displays contradictory features/properties.

2. Where P's account of knowledge fits something that isn't knowledge.

3. Where P knows Knowledge but not by fitting P's account of knowledge.

Let P's account of knowledge be labeled as a Criterion. Three hypothetical situations have to be considered:

Situation 1 finds it conceivable that on P's Criterion, P's attempt to know Knowledge in itself generates contradictions, so P doesn't know Knowledge.

Situation 2 finds it conceivable that on P's Criterion, P's attempt to know Knowledge in itself actually turns out to know Y, and Y ≠ Knowledge, so P doesn't know Knowledge.

Situation 3 finds it conceivable that P actually knows Knowledge, but not through P's Criterion, so P doesn't know that P knows Knowledge.

Each situation is a familiar paradox for epistemology. Unless those three Situations can all be definitively ruled out, no one is able to know knowledge, and hence no one really has any knowledge of anything. However, investigating these situations exposes paradoxes, ruling out knowledge.

Paradox 1. In order for a person to know Knowledge, this person would already have to have the correct Criterion for gaining knowledge of anything. If this person could already comprehend how to have knowledge, this person would already know Knowledge. A person's attempt to know Knowledge therefore generates the contradiction that a person is both knowing Knowledge and not knowing Knowledge. Since (so far as anyone can tell) no person already knows Knowledge, and the contradiction cannot be affirmed, then no one can comprehend how to have knowledge of anything, including Knowledge. Therefore, no knowledge of anything is possible, including knowledge of Knowledge.

Paradox 2. In order for a person P to correctly use a Criterion for knowledge, P must use a Criterion that only approves what is true knowledge and never what is false. However, for P to select the right Criterion, even if P can compare a Criterion against many cases of true knowledge, the amount of true knowledge is potentially infinite, so P cannot know if any Criterion will never approve what is false. Therefore, P doesn't know Knowledge.

Paradox 3. Perhaps a person P actually knows Knowledge, but P doesn't know how this knowledge of Knowledge is possible. No matter what Criterion P appeals to, P may not be able to determine if that Criterion is the exclusive way to know Knowledge, so P cannot know that P knows Knowledge. Even though P knows Knowledge, P won't reliably know that P knows anything else.

These three paradoxes exemplify the classic "problem of the criterion" in distinctive ways, all leading to skepticism.[11]

Due to its skeptical problems and unresolvable paradoxes, grounding epistemology on the mind's inerrant knowledge must suffer from what may be labeled as the generalized problem of the Cartoid and the generalized paradox of the Criterion.

The generalized problem of the Cartoid: Let a "Cartesian factoid," or "Cartoid" for short, be a contingent statement asserting a real matter, that needn't be ever known by anyone, which is inserted into an envisioned situation as a truth. Using a Cartoid to show that knowledge isn't possible is not difficult: pick a Cartoid so that, even though P is justified in truly believing S about X, there is a disconnection between what P justifiably believes and a real X. For any envisioned situation describing a person apparently knowing X through holding a justified true belief, a suitably designed Cartoid can be inserted so that it turns out that this person cannot genuinely know a real X. Hence, no person knows any real X.

The generalized paradox of the Criterion: Only a Criterion tested again known truths should be applied for ascertaining knowledge, but no truths are knowable without a Criterion. Hence, no criterion can be reasonably applied, and no person can know any real X.

Summary

Between the twin problems of the Cartoid and the Criterion, traditional epistemology terminates in skeptical exhaustion. On its own principles, epistemology cannot know knowledge or connect knowledge with static truth and rigid reality.

Knowledge cannot simply be justified true belief so long as knowledge is taken to primarily be propositional statements about "preposed" realities. Epistemology's hope that knowledge of statements will ensure knowledge of realities can secure no way to leap across rationalism's logical and ontological chasm between thoughts and things.

Discerning where pragmatism makes its dissent from traditional views of knowledge brings into clarity the pragmatist stance on key epistemological issues, such as the definition of knowledge, Gettier problems, the mind–world relationship, and realism.

Avoiding the puzzles and paradoxes inherent to traditional epistemology's reliance on rationalism, charted in this chapter, suggests an alternative theory about the knower–known relationship, delineated in the next chapter.

TRANSACTIONAL KNOWLEDGE

Pragmatism rejects the principle of "Inerrant Knowing" and epistemology's self-imposed strictures for knowing knowledge. The appropriate reply to a proffered Gettier problem is to say, "It is irrelevant for knowledge of P that an assertion may claim 'in truth not-P' or 'in truth P.'"

Adding ad-hoc conditions to "justified true belief" won't work so long as rationalism is presumed, because it is too easy to add, "And yet, P is really the case" to a putative knowledge situation. It is that sort of addition which dooms knowledge, just as the thing-in-itself always does. Restoring knowledge requires subtracting aloof truth. Claiming that P is true does not show P, show evidence of P, or show that P pertains to a knowledge situation.

As for the Criterion problem, pragmatism denies that comprehending knowledge rests on any inerrant knowledge. Criteria for methodically justifying knowledge do not have truth conditions. Knowledge criteria are themselves gradually invented, tested, and improved from the course of empirical inquiries, not perfectly known in advance of all inquiry. Any non-rationalistic worldview, particularly one favorable towards empirical science, should take these stances.

Pragmatism relies on a co-respondence theory of knowledge, not a correspondence notion of truth. The knowably real thing must at minimum possess the capacity to respond in anticipatable ways to a learner's exploratory methods of inquiry.

Realizing Realities

For pragmatism, a person can continue to know something until its errancy becomes ascertainably probable, even if conceiving such errancy remains possible. In general, a merely possible truth or falsity cannot negate an actual item of knowledge. Actual knowledge implies known truth, but possible truth or falsity cannot imply actual error or justification failure.

The stubborn proponent of a Gettier problem will insist, "But this isn't about a possible truth, but an actual truth!" That insistence just doubles down on a mere claim offered without evidence, reinvoking the transcendent thing-in-itself. Pragmatism refuses to admit any thing-in-itself to a knowledge situation, so no mere assertion could disturb knowledge. Admirers of Gettier-style arguments strangely imagine that the mere assertion of a truth could properly belong to an empirical situation of potential knowledge.

Even empiricists, still caught up in Kantian categories and dichotomies, may fall into this rationalist trap. To avoid the trap, ask for concrete evidence in a situation of inquiry where knowledge is the goal. If knowledge is not the goal, all manner of hypotheticals can be entertained, as in Gettier pseudo-problems. If knowledge is the goal, then additional evidence in a situation is relevant and the knowing situation is altered; and so, just as pragmatism would expect, reevaluating knowledge is reasonable.

Pragmatism does not reject the rule of non-contradiction within the sphere of empirical inquiry. It is impossible to simultaneously know P and know not-P. But Gettier pseudo-problems fail to include knowledge of, or even evidence of, a P (or not-P) in their hypothetical situations. Those hypotheticals rely on unknowables. Rationalism ensures that it is forever impossible to know P if not-P, regardless of whether there is ever any cognizance of not-P.

Abandoning rationalism means that knowing P at one time is compatible with knowing not-P at another time, just as believing P today but not tomorrow is unremarkable; knowing P better falsifies prior judgments of knowing not-P. This expresses pragmatism's principle of "fallibilism."[1]

Efforts to test acquired knowledge against further events and future outcomes has to presume this fallibilism. According to rationalism, there could be no sense to testing knowledge—true knowledge is necessarily consistent with any possible testing. For rationalism, reasoning mainly proceeds from the known towards the as-yet known. For pragmatism, phases of empirical inquiry may proceed deductively, but acquiring knowledge generally proceeds from the as-yet known to the known, a process called learning. Pragmatism accordingly judges that whatever is really knowable must be responsive to a dynamic process, effecting anticipatable results during the execution of methods of inquiry.

Key tenets to epistemology's grounding in permanence and rationalism can be compared item by item with pragmatism's transactional alternative. Epistemology first:

1. Absolute knowledge is only of the real, and the real is *autontos*, real by itself—so no relations to anything else may essentially alter what it is.

2. Absolute truth primarily concerns the real, not in its relations to other matters, but in its *autontos*, so truth cannot be altered without losing it.

3. Either Absolute truth is identical to, and indistinguishable from, the real—or Absolute truth takes a

form identical to the real. If Absolute truth is entirely identical to the real (truth has substantial identity with the real), then Absolute truth exists independently from any knowledge of it. If Absolute truth takes a form identical to the real, then Absolute truth exists only because of the real, and only accidentally has relations with any knower.

4. Since Absolute knowledge is only of the real, it is therefore only of truth (by substantial identity or by formal identity), and truth admits of no degrees nor changes, so knowledge is digital (1/0) and identical only to itself (1=1).

5. Knowledge about a matter consisting of a set of truths can have degrees only in the aggregate sense that it is possible to know a smaller subset of those truths, and then add knowledge to that subset. But each truth is either known, or it is not; it is impossible for one person to partially know a truth, or to know a truth better or worse than another person.

6. Belief and justification are matters which can have degrees and levels, but knowledge cannot.

7. Having a stronger or weaker degree of belief about an item of knowledge is irrelevant to whether knowledge is possessed by a person.

8. If a person P knows S through justification J, and then later acquires even better justification K for S, that justification improvement cannot alter P's knowledge of S in any way.

9. If person P knows S through justification J, while person Q also knows S but through justification K, and K is a better justification than J, that justification deficit cannot alter P's knowledge of S in any way.

10. Having a better or worse justification for an item of knowledge is irrelevant to whether knowledge is possessed by a person.

11. If something allegedly known is wrong, what makes it wrong is not how strongly it was believed or how well it was justified, but instead how it fails to relate to truth.

12. A reasonable affirmation of knowledge can fail to be actual knowledge without anyone ever finding out. Therefore, so far as any knower can tell, they aren't assuredly knowers, even if they hold justified true beliefs.

Pragmatism reverses these principles by addressing dynamic realities that participate in their knowledge.

12* A reasonable affirmation of knowledge cannot fail to be actual knowledge without anyone ever finding out.

11* If something allegedly known is wrong, what makes it wrong is how strongly it was believed or how well it was justified.

10* Having a better or worse justification for an item of knowledge is relevant to whether knowledge is possessed by a person.

9* If person P knows S through justification J, while person Q also knows S but through justification K, and K is a better justification than J, that justification deficit alters P's knowledge of S.

8* If a person P knows S through justification J, and then later acquires even better justification K for S, that justification improvement can alter P's knowledge of S.

7* Having a stronger or weaker degree of belief about an item of knowledge is relevant to whether knowledge is possessed by a person.

6* Belief and justification are matters which can have degrees and levels, so knowledge has degrees and levels as well.

5* It is possible for one person to know a truth to a certain degree and to partially know a truth, and to know a truth better or worse than another person, because a truth may be more or less adequate about forging and maintaining relations between real matters.

4* Knowledge is primarily of the real in its actual relations, and therefore expresses truths about creating and maintaining dynamic relationships between real interacting matters (the knower, the knowing, and the known). Neither the known, the knowing, nor the knower are unaltered through the knowing process.

3* Truth tracks the forging of relationships between real matters. The nature of a particular relationship determines the specific form that truth's tracking takes, but truth is always about relations with a real knower.

2* Truth primarily concerns the real in its relations, so truth can be altered without losing it.

1* Knowledge is of the real in its relations that are making it what it is.

Whatever is known must be responsive within a justificatory process allowing it to be knowable. This process, for pragmatism, is a two-way dynamic process: realities can and do participate in their realization. Reality need not be known entirely, but something real cannot be forever impervious to attempts at its conceivability and knowability.

Although thinking of a thing does not alter it, realizing its existence does involve it in its modifications, because a real thing is *engaging* with its environs anyways, eliciting consequences that are able to reach the inquirer's solicitations of *searching*. This dynamic relation of transaction, not just reaction or interaction, characterizes knowledge of reality.

Realistic Knowing

Any rationalist can agree that knowing is a process relating to the known. Yet permanence and impassivity must prevail. Rationalism expects the satisfaction of noncontradiction and contingency to keep knowledge realistic. The real maintains intrinsic properties *and* stays substantially unaffected whether known or not.

Pragmatism finds nothing realistic about these two rationalistic conditions placed upon knowledge. When combined, they forbid realism. Realism at minimum expects real things to sustain their properties as they are when known. Irrealism lacks that expectation, letting a thing's properties vary or attributing its properties to a knower's knowing rather than a thing's being. Pragmatism satisfies minimal realism, since the real thing discerned for knowledge is conceived with stable efficacies that are entirely capable of rediscovery. By contrast, the "reals" of rationalism are less reliable. What is so essential must lie beyond effective conceivability and discernability, depriving realistic meaning from an idea of it. What may be so different apart from knowability could not be discoverable either, denying realistic contact with it.

Genuine realism needs no mysterious essences nor unstable manifestations: the real thing as known persists before and after conditions of inquiry confirming its existence. Rationalism instead demands that a thing's reality stays independent from knowledge's confirmation efforts. For rationalism, things and thoughts must remain apart. If knowing affects a thing, only that knowing is truly known and not the thing as it is in itself. Realism, by contrast, finds that the knowable thing is truly real, unable to make sense of a superior reality for unknowables.

Pragmatism does capture the spirit of realism: there are real things ready for adroit inquiries eliciting their natures. Why should a reality worth believing in have to require that belief may never reach it? Rationalism suffers needless anxieties over empirical inquiry, hypostatizing the purity of true conceptions into truths untainted by discovery. Pragmatism does not hold that something that has not been discerned from inquiry cannot be conceivably real. Pragmatism *does* say that something that has not been conceived as discernible through inquiry has not yet been conceived as real.

"Knowledge is of the real in its relations making it what it is." This final tenet (1*) above commits pragmatism to realism concerning knowledge, from the conceptual stage to the confirmable stage. Conceptions are clear and realistic by conceiving an entity in terms of effects making discernible differences in practice.

Recall Peirce's principle: "Consider what effects, that might conceivably have practical bearings, we conceive the object of our conception to have. Then, our conception of these effects is the whole of our conception of the object."[2] This principle ensures than a concept is realizable, rather than just ideational. Ideations abound and concepts proliferate, but realism sets a higher standard for credible reference. The notion that ideas only linked to other ideas (by synonym, definition, connotation, formulation, and so on) can be meaningful enough to refer to actualities is a view associated with idealism, not realism.

Knowing is not basically intuitive, didactic, spectorial, ideational, or testimonial. Familiar acquired knowledge may adopt those formats. Impressions of unbidden thoughts, repetitions of another's verities, envisionings of simple scenes, followings of related ideas, and statements of recalled events are at most potential material for further learning and teaching. Affirming knowledge by those means are the rewards of membership in a community of knowledge, knowledge we did little or nothing to create.

Verity attaches to "facts" because they are assertible matters relevant to ongoing activities, noticeable for their meaningful leadings to further matters of interest. They are, in a sense, "the taken-for-granted," but they are never "granted for the taking." No fact is "given" to apprehension or cognition, and nothing "fact-shaped" is ever presented to the senses. The basic reason why neither you nor I know that "the cat is on the mat" or "a barn is by the road" (illustrations picked for epistemology enthusiasts) is because we haven't been looking for that cat, or exploring that barn. Thinking a thought by itself isn't knowing anything. Pragmatism advises that if you are a thinking thing, act like it. Learning arises from trying, and knowing emerges from stubborn experiments in learning.

Pragmatism finds that more complex matters require the collective methodical investigations fostered within "communities of inquiry," to use Peirce's label.[3] This "community of inquiry" is the smallest unit for situating knowledge about this or that subject matter. Individual knowers access knowledge only by membership or followership. Furthermore, only communities of inquiry are responsible for their methods, as methodologies (including inferential, instrumental, and experimental techniques) develop right along with empirical inquiries so that confidence in methods tracks the credibility of discoveries.

There is no criterial problem of circularity to this twinned method–discovery system, unless rationalism is readmitted. Knowledge tends to grow. The prior justification of methodology rests on past discoveries, but methods are tested again in the search for further findings. Examples of data going unquestioned for too long, or scientists getting dogmatic about methods, are illustrations of methodology's resilience, not counterexamples refuting communal inquiry. Inventing a whole methodology in order to justify preferred claims is the fraudulent game of charlatanry and pseudo-science.

Knowledge rests on method, the path towards objectivity. Sincerities and certainties seem like unchallengeable verities, and one's "truths" say plenty about oneself. As a knower, however, one is oriented by methodology, not subjectivity. Pragmatism offers two regulative criteria (not a "definition") of guidance for an individual knower.

Person P knows a real X where

(a) P has methodically become justified in making a description D about a specific X, and

(b) P asserts D about that X due to that methodical process.

Knowledge, for an individual, is justified assertion. Adding that knowledge "must be true" is superfluous and misleading; knowledge's verity is beheld with its methodical confirmation.

Specifications about proper applications of particular methods falls to the purview of inquiry communities. Since inquiry communities are responsible for their methodologies, their collective affirmations are the ultimate justifications backing any particular claims to knowledge. Knowledge in general is justified affirmation.

Pragmatism expects the many areas of knowledge to display contradictions and incoherencies between them, yet this situation is no refutation, since rationalism's strictures do not apply. Asking inquiry communities to seek reconciliations, coherences, and syntheses of their knowledge is entirely reasonable. Pragmatism urges pluralism and contextualism in the areas of social epistemology and philosophy of science.

Futures for Truth

Pragmatism acquired its notoriety with its controversial meaning for truth while undertaking a confrontation with rationalism. Rationalism aligns truth directly and statically with reality, leaving the growth of knowledge as a conundrum. To philosophically explain knowledge, truth must be conceived as primarily prospective, not circumspective or retrospective.

Looking back, established bodies of knowledge are historical from today's vantage, but they were learned from fresh inquiries of their time. Looking around, knowledgeable communities are plentiful for offering truths, but mutual adjustments and reconciliations await further investigations. More truths, and better truths, anticipate practical trials so that reals can get realized. Pragmatism mediates concepts of reality and truth through knowing, the methodical processes of inquiry.

This mediation between truth and reality is exemplified in Peirce's blunt statements in "How to Make Our Ideas Clear":

> The opinion which is fated to be ultimately agreed to by all who investigate, is what we mean by the truth, and the object represented in this opinion is the real. That is the way I would explain reality. But it may be said that this view is directly opposed to the abstract definition which we have given of reality, inasmuch as it makes the characters of the real depend on what is ultimately thought about them. But the answer to this is that, on the one hand, reality is independent, not necessarily of thought in general, but only of what you or I or any finite number of [inquirers] may think about it; and that, on the other hand, though the object of the final opinion depends on what that opinion is, yet what that opinion is does not depend on what you or I or any man thinks.[4]

Here, Peirce is only addressing a conception of truth that itself passes his test of clear conception, not some other unclear connotation of truth. This is philosophy, not lexicography.

"The opinion which is fated to be ultimately agreed to by all who investigate, is what we mean by the truth."
—Charles Sanders Peirce

Peirce's conception of truth as that knowledge which would satisfy tests of indefinitely prolonged inquiry is an effective conception of truth that makes a difference to practical inquiry. It makes such a vast difference, that only genuine communities of inquiry form around a shared commitment to such strenuous truth, such as investigatory disciplines and scientific fields.

Peirce's meaning for reality is similarly delimited to that sphere, after the Kantian thing-in-itself gets eliminated and reality turns out to be where it always was, inviting engagements with its activities. Pragmatism's theory of knowledge about the world created by inquirers at work within that world promises that the triadic relationship of [Reals, Truths, Knowings] within practical achievements must affect all three components.

Letting rationalistic questions divide apart [Reals, Truths, Knowings] for separate treatment lends the appearance of paradox to pragmatism. On the one hand, things are realistically conceived prior to a prediction of their discovery when inquiry is initiated, but on the other hand, reality is projected far out at the culmination of maximal inquiries not yet imaginable. When does pragmatism want a thing to be real—before or after knowing it? Peirce does encourage a view of the process of knowing as never ending, and never needing to end.[5] Where does the truth lie—does the truth already exist for discovery, or does the truth only exist when inquiries are exhausted?

Such interrogations are false to pragmatism. They try to metaphysically conceive truth and reality apart from knowing, as a-temporally fixed matters. Pragmatism instead takes knowledge (and true knowing, and known reals) to be fallible and provisional. Fallibilism about truth is the sounder realism, and idealism is banished. Peirce does not claim that truth is limited to whatever actual inquirers manage to discover before their expiration or extinction. No pragmatist asserts that realities cannot exist unless mentalities encounter them. It is a mistake to assimilate pragmatism's view of truth to idealism, especially since it asserts that anything actual must be conceived realistically.

Discovery does require inquiry, nonetheless. "The True" is a regulative ideal for inquiry in general, expecting "the real" discovered so far to withstand any amount of potential investigation in the future. This pragmatist conception of "The True" makes a difference to empirical methodologies and communities of inquiry applying them, preventing halts to thought in arbitrary dogma. Today's knowledge is of hypothesized entities that are, so far, credibly real, so asserting their actuality is to assert truths as we know them. But their credibility is lent "on credit" which can be withdrawn due to future improved inquiries not yet conducted.

To admit that today's truths will probably be replaced by superior richer truths only sounds contradictory on rationalism's dictum that "truth tomorrow means no truth today." Fallibilism is not relativism or irrealism—it stands as reasonably realistic. Although any theory could require revision or replacement in the future, this displays knowledge's growth, not its death. There can be no "pessimistic induction" advising skepticism and irrealism about today's theories. Petulant incredulity towards still-confirmable things is unreasonable, and premature incredulity towards to-be-confirmed things is irrational.

Pragmatism's optimism about knowledge is not grounded on the idealistic principle that The Real is known. Optimism is instead based on the confirmed knowability of many reals, the intelligent discovery of innumerable actualities.

Truth tracks the forging of relationships between real matters. Mmethodical justification is the process of forging the transactional relationship of co-respondence between the knower and the known. Those co-respondences yield knowledge of actualities, but concrete propositions never lose the plasticity of empirical testability and fallibility. Known beliefs remain propositional, in the sense of "proposals" intending the future, not the static "propositions" of statements enjoying final truth. Dewey critiqued the rationalist view of propositions in this way:

> [T]he primary common assumption of both realistic and idealistic conceptions is that a statement by its nature implies an assertion of its own truth. No,

replies the pragmatist, a statement, a proposition, in just the degree in which it has a genuinely intellectual quality, implies a doubt concerning its own truth and a search for truth, an inquiry for it. The proposition which asserts or assumes its own truth is either a sheer prejudice, a congealed dogmatism; or else it is not an intellectual or logical proposition at all, but simply a linguistic memorandum . . . [A proposition] is a hypothesis concerning some state of affairs; that it is of its nature to be doubtful, not assured, of truth; and that its assertion of its own truth is only conditional: that it is a means of setting on foot activities of inquiry which will test the worth of its claim. Truth, then, can exist only in the testing of the claim, in making good through the subsequent acts it prescribes.[6]

This is a consequentialist theory of truth. It fulfills the expectations of idealism for thought's efficacy in knowledge, while satisfying the demands of realism about the objectivity attainable with knowledge. Science is now set up as an exemplar of objective knowledge, rather than mathematics. Only rationalistic strictures have allowed philosophy to separate idealism and realism into opposed worldviews, unable to even view the same world.

Dewey continues,

The pragmatic theory thus claims faithfully to
represent the spirit, that is the method, of science,
which (1) regards all statements as provisional or
hypothetical till submitted to experimental test;
(2) endeavors to frame its statements in terms
which will themselves indicate the procedures
required to test them; and (3) never forgets that
even its assured propositions are but the summaries
of prior inquiries and testings, and therefore subject
to any revision demanded by further inquiries. . . .
[W]ith this change propositions get a future outlook
and reference, while the orthodox notion makes
them refer to antecedent conditions. To realist and
idealist alike truth (or falsity) is a property which
exists ready-made in the intellectual assertion. What
is done with the proposition, what happens from its
use, the differences it makes in further experience—
these are all irrelevant. The pragmatist says that
since every proposition is a hypothesis referring
to an inquiry still to be undertaken (a proposal
in short) its truth is a matter of its career, of its
history: that it becomes or is made true (or false)
in process of fulfilling or frustrating in use its own
proposal.[7]

Summary

For pragmatism, truth is far more consequential than rationalism could ever admit. "Truth" is a label, not a referent. It is the most important label that any product of thought could aspire to attaining.

Truth is adjectival: judgments turn out to be more or less true due to assessed consequences making a difference for life. Truth is adverbial: judgments successfully tested by dynamic mentality through practical trial are veritably affirmable. Truly affirmable judgments are reliable for guiding innumerable further activities that enliven and enrich our world.

ECOLOGICAL MENTALITY

Philosophies before pragmatism have sought alternatives to Cartesianism and its irreconcilable dualisms between experience and reason, and between body and mind. Paths away from Descartes were made easier and straighter by relying on lingering tenets of permanence. The preservation of privileged mental responsibilities remained paramount, to keep humanity elevated far above all animals, and to elevate philosophy above all other areas of knowledge, especially the sciences. Modern and postmodern philosophies retreated to the mind, as the last refuge for disciplinary knowledge, a knowledge of knowledge itself, the sort of knowledge that no other field could duplicate or replace.

Having expelled natural history, biology, anthropology, psychology, and any behavioral and social science, academic philosophies erected high walls around the mind to forever prevent invasion and integration. Alternatives to Descartes mostly reinvented rationalism.

Philosophies of permanence, along with most philosophies of impermanence, contended for primacy in their chosen isolation by contesting the nature of mind. Previous chapters have integrated mind within pragmatism's theory of knowledge and truth. The last bastion of resistance to pragmatism is precisely where post-Cartesian philosophy carried it away, the mind itself. Pragmatism finds that mentality is selective, purposive, ecological, and social, with nothing more about "mind" to have to mind.

Mind–Matter Mutuality

Post-Cartesian philosophies proposed revised conceptions of mind without abandoning views such as "the mind holds certainties unobtainable from perception," or "the mind remains distinct from physical matters," or "minds stay individualized while externally related," or "minds make choices aloof from causal forces." Above all, the mind's nature seeks knowledge, to know truths. A philosopher denying this purpose of mind has no knowledgeable mind to heed, committing a self-refutation more devastating than any fallacy. Knowledge, and hence philosophy itself, was at stake. The world supplies reality enough. The mind must do the rest in order to possess knowledge.

The legacy of Descartes assigned twinned responsibilities to the mind: it attends to mind-independent realities, and it independently minds those realities. Aloof independence is hardly a propitious setting for cooperation. Pragmatism does agree that mind has better work to do than knowing just mind, adding that this productive work is precisely what allows mind to be known. Descartes held that the mind always knows itself best, better than the world. Pragmatism finds that the mind gradually learns about itself by learning from the world in which mind is embedded.

Distinctive modes of centralized and organized activity distinguish mentality from the rest of actuality. In order to accurately identify those modes, and their orientations towards objectivity, we must directly address the issue of independence. Cartesianism's legacy licensed the conflation of four distinguishable meanings for an "independence" to a reality: (a) not dependent on mind's consciousness (a material cause); (b) not dependent on mind's concepts (a formal cause); (c) not dependent on mind's knowing (an efficient cause); and (d) not dependent on mind's regimentation (a final cause).

These tenets can be contradicted, but diametric opposition was never in pragmatism's plans. No denial could suffice to reconcile Cartesian dualisms. Simply reuniting contrary views would inflate mind to cosmic proportions or consign a mind to solipsist prison. Instead, by reversing that order of (a) to (d), pragmatism treats telic relationality as the basis for reuniting mind and world. Organizing mentality effectively constructs a knowable world through conceptual inferences requiring conscious attention.

Duality should be replaced by mutuality. Interdependency is the validation, not a subjugation, for both mentality and physicality. Mentality without capability is vacuous, physicality without potency is void. Nothing therefore remains to keep mind and reality apart. Their ontological commonality lies in processive activity comprising all actuality. Classifying pragmatism as either an idealism or a realism on traditional metaphysical terms is a mistake. Pragmatism expressly rejected those terms. Worldly matters subsist for activities having stability; mental functions persist for activities having reliability. Mentality operates within reality. Dynamic interactivity characterizes all.

Neither mentality nor materiality must be reduced to the other. Mentality finds the world to be endlessly discoverable, and reality generates mentality from its boundless energy. This "generation" is akin to the way that a crystal grows from a solution or a plant grows from the soil, without any mysterious ontological gap between process and product. Biology, not logic, supplies the key terms for comprehending how organic mentality displays its capacities for exploring and modifying its environment.[1] The mind is not reproducing internal models of externalities. Remodeling external matters *is* the mind thinking. Inference, reasonableness, and logicality grew from mentality's strivings for precise and reliable control over manifold conditions and outcomes.

Rationalism insists that what lies beyond and what lies behind has a separable and more substantial reality, assigning a derivative and dependent status to whatever grows and learns. Pragmatism assigns no ontological priority in any direction. Interdependent modification through change is all that could be said to be fundamental. Therefore, "the mind" has no permanent attributes or substantial existence all its own. Operations and functions of what was "the mind" are better attributable to that feature of reality hereby called "mentality." Mind is not something responsible for mentality—there is *only* mentality, wherever reality permits its characteristic activity.

To refuse to observe real mentality within patterned processes of dynamic reality is to presume the very dualism that a metaphysician should have to prove. Pragmatism has nothing to prove here except to show how to avoid that presumptive fallacy, a false start still prevalent even in science. Dewey points out,

> The dualism is found today even among those who have abandoned its earlier manifestations. It is

shown in separations made between the structural and the functional; between the brain and the rest of the body; between the central nervous system and the vegetative nervous system and viscera; and, most fundamentally, between the organism and the environment. For the first of each of these pairs of terms—structure, brain, organism—retains something of the isolation and alleged independence that used to belong to the "soul and the mind," and later to "consciousness."[2]

This worldview endorsed by pragmatism is not a "dual aspect" theory of mind and matter. Physicality and mentality are not aspects of some mysterious ultimacy, but modes of one and the same real activity. There is nothing "behind" mind and matter. Both consist entirely of processive activity.

Nor does pragmatism endorse panpsychism. A functionally perspectival view of mentality does not need to imbue all physicality with a degree of mentality. Anything real, whether more of the physical or of the mental, occurs in ontologically neutral processes having the form of situational durations, or "events." Within reality, time–space–energy are fused and inseparable.[3] From the standpoint of an organism embedded in this dynamical cosmos, physicality and mentality are distinguishable and describable according to their different functionalities. Mentality has, in general, modes of activity that have evolved to be particularly conducive to self-organizing and systemic growing.

This cosmological interdependency of mentality and physicality resolves metaphysical conundrums lingering in the West since Democritus and Plato. The installation of consciousness during the rise of European modernity as a proxy for the unnatural soul delayed that resolution. At long last, the idea of substance had to be overthrown.

In the tradition of Baruch Spinoza, Johann Gottfried von Herder, and Friedrich Wilhelm Joseph Schelling, Peirce did not connect mind and matter with rigid relations. He instead fused them together within patterned processes.

> . . . all mind is directly or indirectly connected with all matter, and acts in a more or less regular way; so that all mind more or less partakes of the nature of matter. Hence, it would be a mistake to conceive of the psychical and the physical aspects of matter as two aspects absolutely distinct. Viewing a thing from the outside, considering its relations of action and reaction with other things, it appears as matter. Viewing it from the inside, looking at its immediate character as feeling, it appears as consciousness. These two views are combined when we remember that mechanical laws are nothing but acquired

habits, like all the regularities of mind, including the
tendency to take habits, itself . . .[4]

That "subjectivity" of mind can no longer inflate into
its own substantial being. Dewey's account of this process pragmatism situates the mental, like the biological,
amidst the physical.

> The distinction between physical, psycho-physical,
> and mental is thus one of levels of increasing
> complexity and intimacy of interaction among
> natural events. The idea that matter, life and mind
> represent separate kinds of Being is a doctrine that
> springs, as so many philosophic errors have sprung,
> from a substantiation of eventual functions. . . .
> "Matter," or the physical, is a character of events when
> they occur at a certain level of interaction. It is not
> itself an event or existence; the notion that while
> "mind" denotes essence, "matter" denotes existence is
> superstition. It is more than a bare essence; for it is a
> property of a particular field of interacting events.[5]

Features or characters of mind, differentiable from
worldly matters as expected for a pluralistic cosmos, do
not merit independent metaphysical status. There is no
separate ontology just for mind or consciousness.

Conscious Relationality

William James concurred with this worldview assigning functional relationality to mentality. Against idealism's claim that mind organizes perceptions with ideal relations to produce an immaterial field of consciousness, he pointed out how relations among perceived things are equally phenomenally present. Empiricists agreeing with idealism that consciousness consists only of ideal copies rather than material objects are never able to produce any evidence for this spectral sheen. Pointing a finger up at the moon is not a gesture to something within one's consciousness or mind, and the moon's brightness is a meaningful property of your situation with the moon, not an inner quality lacking functionality.

That pernicious "scheme–content" dichotomy is a perennial problem. Idealists and empiricists each isolate one factor to ordinary experience in order to deny its presence in the world. Idealists abstract out the relatedness to experience and then credit all relationality to transcendental mind. Empiricists abstract out the qualitativeness to experience and then credit all quality to perception untouched by mind.

Both camps cling to an unreal "thought-in-itself" and then deny that the external world is directly experienced, leaving it as a mysterious "thing-in-itself." For pragmatism, that thing called "the concept" is a grammatical fiction, not really bearing any fixed self-sufficient meaning. That thing called a "qualia" is an introspective fiction, not really presenting any static non-intentional intensity.[6] The experienced world is qualitatively conceivable as we attend to things around us, not to illusions within us.

After dispelling versions of that "thought-in-itself" with an honest examination of ordinary lived experience— what James called his radical empiricism[7]—"consciousness" disappears and one is immediately confronted with the experienced world, where it always has been. Whatever consciousness would still be, it persists within this flowing attentiveness within the world, instead of spectrally hovering above it or entertaining imagistic duplicates of it. Consciousness never deserved an ontological status of its own.

In his 1904 article "Does Consciousness Exist?" James cannot empirically discover what this supposed "stuff" of consciousness could be. He concludes,

> I believe that "consciousness," when once it has evaporated to this estate of pure diaphaneity, is on the point of disappearing altogether. It is the name of a nonentity, and has no right to a place among first principles. Those who still cling to it are clinging to a mere echo, the faint rumor left behind by the disappearing "soul" upon the air of philosophy. . . .

The instant field of the present is at all times what I call the "pure" experience. It is only virtually or potentially either object or subject as yet. For the time being, it is plain, unqualified actuality, or existence, a simple *that*. . . . Consciousness connotes a kind of external relation, and does not denote a special stuff or way of being.[8]

Attentive awareness, what the pragmatists treated as consciousness, is a particularly focused portion of ongoing experienced reality. Consciousness must not be equated with that entire phenomenal realm. Both objective world and subjective mind emerge from this field of experience-able reality.

While consistent with minimal realism, this world-view is not a metaphysical realism, because reality no-where is utterly unlike mentality.[9] This worldview cannot be a metaphysical idealism either, because mentality only participates with the rest of reality to a limited extent. Connective and interactive relationality binds all. Ideal-ists rightly take all that activity of relating and intending to be the activity of mind, but they mistakenly suppose that "the mind" has to be something more than just the relational activity itself. Nothing lies behind or beyond ex-perience as a "thinker-in-itself," such as a transphenom-enal subject, the unifying "I," or the transcendental ego, to perpetually bind the phenomenal realm together.

Dewey agreed whole-heartedly with James's dismissal of consciousness as a mental substance. He put it this way: "Mind is primarily a verb. It denotes all the ways in which we deal consciously and expressly with the situations in which we find ourselves. Unfortunately, an influential manner of thinking has changed modes of action into an underlying substance that performs the activities in question. It has treated mind as an independent entity, which attends, purposes, cares, and remembers."[10]

There is nothing metaphysically independent or self-sufficient to be discerned about mentality, for a dynamically processive reality consisting of innumerable kinds of shifting events. Only variations among functional stabilities and instabilities distinguish their lasting or fleeting influences. Experience originally arrives in ever-arriving compositions of situational durations. Nothing additional is needed to shape a spatiotemporal world. Within that one world, human mentality engages capacities for adjusting our habitual behaviors and hence for modifying the encountered world.

Dewey again:

> The first great consideration is that life goes on in an environment; not merely in but because of it, through interaction with it. No creature lives merely under its skin; its subcutaneous organs are means of

connection with what lies beyond its bodily frame, and to which, in order to live, it must adjust itself, by accommodation and defense but also by conquest. . . . The career and destiny of a living being are bound up with its interchanges with its environment.[11]

Mind is always interrelated with and within the world. Inconstant realities requiring attentive management *and* persistent mentality is a dynamic aspect of ongoing reality.[12] Human mentality develops its own habitual stabilities to manage the conduct of our practices. Permanencies are not needed. Seemingly static features of mind, suspended in reflective abstraction, have only a formulaic status without concrete import. The idealized concept, that simple essence, or whatever populates metaphysical fantasies about mind, are examples of that thought-in-itself to be exorcized from philosophy. Meanings are not trapped inside consciousness for contemplating. Meanings are out in the world where valued activities are happening.

Mentality is about telic relationality embedded within processive reality. Among the innumerable kinds of purposive relationalities for mentality, complex forms serve as signs for suitably sentient organisms. All thought, according to Peirce, consists of the enchained meanings to signs. There cannot be anything more to consciousness than that.

Inconstant realities requiring attentive management *and* persistent mentality is a dynamic aspect of ongoing reality.

> . . . in what does the reality of the mind consist? We
> have seen that the content of consciousness, the
> entire phenomenal manifestation of mind, is a
> sign resulting from inference. Upon our principle,
> therefore, that the absolutely incognizable does not
> exist, so that the phenomenal manifestation of a
> substance is the substance, we must conclude that
> the mind is a sign developing according to the laws
> of inference. . . . consciousness is sometimes used
> to signify the *I think*, or unity in thought; but the
> unity is nothing but consistency, or the recognition
> of it. Consistency belongs to every sign, so far
> as it is a sign; and therefore every sign, since it
> signifies primarily that it is a sign, signifies its own
> consistency.[13]

Although it is of the nature of a sign to participate
in representation about some object, Peirce's theory of
mind is far from traditional representationalism. A sign
offering mere qualitative or isomorphic similarity conveys
little actionable information. The highest grade of sign, a
symbol, need not imitate or resemble an object at all. Its
function is not to remake an acquaintance, but to facilitate
an anticipation of what happens from interacting with the
object. Interoperability is memorable for a practical mind;
concepts are retained to connect sensibility with habituality. As Peirce wrote, "The elements of every concept enter

into logical thought at the gate of perception and make their exit at the gate of purposive action; and whatever cannot show its passports at both those two gates is to be arrested as unauthorized by reason."[14]

A meaningful conception of an object cannot fail to engage that real object, because only that engagement supplies the concept's meaning. Neither intentionality nor reference need to be mysteries, because sense is assuredly linked to preference. Where there is no intended selection among interactions with an object, then there is no reference to it at all.

Embodied Mentality

Cartesianism still pervades too much psychology and philosophy of mind by demanding a narrow localization of rationality, a priority for self-consciousness's powers, and a quest for veritable representations of the external world. However, all biological evidence points to a very different portrait of mentality and intelligence. The brain exhibits much dedicated modular architecture, but massive parallel and networked processing is dominant. The brain is not hierarchical, but more democratic and interdependent. Nerve centers across the brains are intricately interconnected with each other. Most any part of the brain has some direct or indirect systemic link to every other part of the brain.

There is no inner Cartesian theater where all information is gathered and simultaneously experienced. Experience at best displays rough continuities. There is no executive command center giving orders to the rest of the brain. Deliberation at best guides habitual motor action. Ordinary cognition does not primarily aim at static representation in general, but rather dynamic adequacy in specific situations.

The Cartesian claim that mind and body are entirely different is demonstrably false. The vast similarities between the twin functionalities of mentality and neurology indicate their embodied interdependence and cofunctionality.[15]

Thought activity and nerve activity both have temporal durations. They are both found in localized living organisms rather than diffused throughout nature. They both consist of relational continuities rather than atomic accumulations. They are both dynamic rather than static. They both display growth and decay. They both function in attending to practical dealings with the environment. And, they both primarily aim at maintaining the organism's well-being. Even the most "subjective" parts of consciousness, such as the flow of feelings and qualities noticeable in self-consciousness, are features of the dynamically functional flow of thought.

Pragmatism does not seek to "reduce" felt qualities to nervous activity or anything else to prove that they are natural. The metaphysical formula demanding identity of all properties for genuine identity is unscientific and unnecessary. Functional consistency is quite sufficient. Where two phenomena are entirely correlated and display the same functionalities, the two phenomena are rightly regarded as the same natural process from different perspectives. Qualitative feelings happen where nervous systems achieve certain degrees of complexity. The lived experience supplied by cognition reflects its neurological basis.

Rationalist philosophies point to features of experience or thought allegedly lacking dynamic functionality or integration with action. However, such supposedly "pure" or "inert" features (sense data, intense qualia, and the like) are only "detectable" through reflective abstraction from the ordinary flow of active experience. What has to be created through cognition cannot be attributed to "original" experience.

The brain rapidly merges diverse streams of stimuli from all sources in order to guide effective action in the lived moment. All cognitive processes (and hence all conscious experiences too) are fusings of information about external sensations, motor control processes, and internal feedback from the body. There is nothing like pure sensation, no pure will, and no pure feeling. There are no dichotomies between sensation, emotion, and reason. These aspects and phases of cognition work together as they guide behavior.

Sensationalism and associationism are inadequate theories of experience because organic circuits create new meaningful wholes that are not merely sums or sequences of their parts. The circuit of perception, action, and consequence develops an enlarging fusion: (1) the meaning of a perception includes a prior action done to gain that perception, such as the turning of the gaze towards an object; (2) the meaning of the action includes both a desire (to touch that object) and more perception (to guide the reaching); and (3) the meaning of the consequences of the touching includes the guided action of touching.

To illustrate, suppose that a child first touches a fascinating flame. The felt pain from touching a hot object is not just felt pain, but the pain of *touching that object*. The next time the child sees the flame, she sees a *hot* flame, and if she reaches for that flame again, fascination has been replaced by wariness as she *reaches for a painful touch*. From then on, for that child, an idea of touching that flame contains the idea of encountering pain, and reaching habits are modified accordingly.[16]

In general, most of the meaning to perceiving things consists of habitual anticipations of potential reactions upon dealing with those things. Organic circuits result in holistic organic wholes of experience. Experience is thoroughly imbued with prospective values of action. That is why we directly experience meanings and values in the world around us.

If meanings or values were only interior mental events or states, then our experience of an external object would be stereoscopic, a sort of double perception. We would observe the external object as a meaningless material thing, and simultaneously observe it as a useful object, as if one "eye" saw the world as it is, while another "eye" saw objects as meaningful and valuable. Does lived experience ever seem like this? Hardly. We immediately and directly observe significant, meaningful, and valuable objects without any double "vision" or contrast between an external world and an internal world.

Meanings and values are where they appear to be: embodied in the things that we know how to approach, engage with, and use. Pragmatism hardly treats these two matters differently, since meanings are valuable leadings towards ends and values are the meant results from doings. Meanings and values are instances of achieved practical knowledge through learning. Knowledge is built up from our experimental attempts to productively manage our deliberate modifications to the environment.

Static representationalism, correspondence theories of knowledge, and Cartesian materialism are not viable theories of mentality and intelligence. Minds are not isolated or aloof from each other; the reason why minds are interactive is because they are always interrelated. Mentality is thoroughly networked, whenever and wherever synchronizing brains are coordinating action through communing and communication. Therefore, most of intelligence's effectiveness arises within communities learning and preserving collective skills and practices.

Our kind of mentality is dependent on our evolved brains and developed intelligence. Cognitive functions involve brain functions, either of single or multiple brains, in the course of sentient conduct. However, it is a mistake to assume that mentality is localized to just the brain or some region of the brain. Neurons are all about systemic communication, across synapses and across spaces between individuals. Many cognitive functions, and all higher cognitive functions, only operate through brains in communication with each other about the common environment. Meanings are embedded in the dynamic relationships and connections, not the final terminations. As Hilary Putnam emphasized, "meanings ain't in the *head*."[17]

Human minds are differentiable since their streams of meaningful experience have separate organic embodiments and particular concerns. Yet there is nothing metaphysically dualistic about this observation, as Dewey explains.

> Experience when it happens has the same
> dependence upon objective natural events, physical
> and social, as has the occurrence of a house. It has
> its own objective and definitive traits; these can be
> described without reference to a self, precisely as a
> house is of brick, has eight rooms, etc., irrespective

of whom it belongs to. Nevertheless, just as for some purposes and with respect to some consequences, it is all important to note the added qualification of personal ownership of real property, so with "experience" . . . it is not exact or relevant to say "I experience" or "I think." "It" experiences or is experienced, "it" thinks or is thought, is a juster phrase. Experience, a serial course of affairs with their own characteristic properties and relationships, occurs, happens, and is what it is. Among and within these occurrences, not outside of them nor underlying them, are those events which are denominated selves.[18]

Experience is among the organic features of lifeforms, and selves emerge from enriched experiences. On Dewey's terms, this is hardly different from pointing out how corn stalks showered with rain will rise tall and yield ears of corn. Shall we conclude that stalks can't be of the same earth, or that corn hides an essence utterly unlike soils from which they grew?

Summary

The organism's effective coordination of efforts to modify its environment (natural and social) exemplifies cognition.

Pragmatism has always refused to treat brain cells as the exclusive place where cognitive meaning is enacted. Neurons are involved with, but not entirely constitutive of, cognition. Neuroscience properly studies the interrelated processes of brain activity, including synchronized mental activity functioning through multiple brains simultaneously. Still, cognitive neuroscience cannot help explain the processes of learning and knowing by referencing brain activity alone in isolation from its environing context.

Biology cannot study life with utter disregard for the environment. Nervous networks, just as any biological system, must not be studied any differently. The same goes doubly for the functions in which such systems take part, such as cognition.

Cognition, therefore, is not to be solely done within the head; cognition should be understood in terms of life, practical activity, and living within habitats. Perception and memory must be understood in terms of their contribution to situation-appropriate behavior under the pressure of real-time interactions with environing matters. Grounding mind in biology takes life seriously. The function of the mind is to guide action.

SOCIETY, SELF, AND MIND

Self and society both evolved gradually in concert together from the growing communal relations characteristic of the *Homo* genus ancestors down to *Homo sapiens*. Among our species, the established sociality of a community is responsible for the rapid socialization and enculturation of each new generation. Selves are not born; they are nurtured and trained.

Individuality, like mentality, is a developed social facility, not a biological or metaphysical category. No one is born as a thinking thing or a personal self. Humanity is a thoroughly symbolic species, but our symbols are never trapped inside spectral minds. Symbolization is exactly and only where mentality is functioning, among coordinating and cooperating people. Communication is a prominent feature of all that communing.

One learns how to be an individual only within a community. Flock, herd, or pack behavior isn't sufficient. Highly communal species—one thinks of chimps, gorillas, dolphins, and elephants—treat members of their kind as unique individuals.[1] Thinking of oneself as an individual, that capacity for self-awareness, comes with the high intelligence for regarding others as individuals too.

Social Cognition

Where in the world are minds? A modern problem of philosophy is the "problem of other minds," a special case of the general problem of knowing the "external" world after the mind is cast as the "internal" world. Idealists, phenomenologists, realists, and empiricists all encounter this problem. In Bertrand Russell's version, "there seems no reason to believe that we are ever acquainted with other people's minds, seeing that these are not directly perceived."[2]

If minds have discrete and separate existences—just like souls, according to Western Christianity—then minds have no direct contact, and a thought cannot be simultaneously shared. For this dualism, other minds are far more inaccessible than external objects. That must be, because experience supplies ideas of objects, but no amount of experience reaches another mind. Philosophers and psychologists beholden to the Cartesian legacy first assume that all minds are strictly individuated entities.

Cartesianism takes one's own mind to be known best, so any knowledge about other minds is dependent on one's conception of one's self as a mind. During the twentieth century, materialism reinforced this presumption. The school of "Cartesian materialism," as philosopher Daniel Dennett labeled it, continued to maintain that the brain supplies what we know best: our inner veridical experience of our own mind.[3]

The methodological individualism of modern Cartesianism erects insurmountable obstacles for explaining how minds attain mutual understanding and coordination. Each of us would have to theoretically project another mind of the same sort that we take ourselves to already have. This amounts to a radically individualistic presumption that self-knowledge of one's mind is both logically and developmentally prior to knowledge of other minds. Cartesian individualism encouraged investigators to experimentally isolate subjects to discern their capacities as lone thinkers and agents.

Eliminating the inner mind from scientific consideration did not circumvent this Cartesianism. For example, B. F. Skinner's methodological individualism regarded all social entities and events to be entirely explicable in terms of aggregate actions of agents. This behaviorism never regarded the cognition of others' minds as a serious possibility, instead taking knowledge of others to be anticipations of their observable behaviors.[4]

The alternative to methodological individualism is sociological mentality: minding others is the only way to develop and exhibit one's own mind. Social cognition about group activities must be essential to mental growth. That is a fact largely unappreciated by both philosophy and psychology during most of the twentieth century, though Jean Piaget and Lev Vygotsky did go far in that direction.[5]

Dewey and Mead went the farthest, offering empirical-based theories of childhood learning through social cognition. Humans are hence able to treat each other as selves because of their intense sociality. Neither selfhood or society have any prior logical or ontological status. One did not generate the other or arise from the other. Mead explained,

> The self, as that which can be an object to itself, is essentially a social structure, and it arises in social experience. After a self has arisen, it in a certain sense provides for itself its social experiences, and so we can conceive of an absolutely solitary self. But it is impossible to conceive of a self arising outside of social experience.[6]

"The self, as that which can be an object to itself, is essentially a social structure, and it arises in social experience."
—George Herbert Mead

Mead and Dewey accordingly asserted that individual psychology cannot be the primary way to study human mentality. At most, individual psychology is physiological and neurological research available for social theorizing, or individual psychology is the study of abnormal behavior too unpredictable to explain social phenomena.

Sociology must be liberated from Cartesianism. Individualizing all mind was the fallacy at the root of modern political and economic theory as well. People are not atomized agents acting only from self-interest. Human psychology is sociological. Dewey stated,

> From the point of view of the psychology of behavior all psychology is either biological or social psychology. And if it still be true that man is not only an animal but a social animal, the two cannot be dissevered when we deal with man.[7]

Regrettably, the social behaviorism of Dewey and Mead was largely ignored by subsequent academic psychology, and its tenets had to be experimentally rediscovered over the past thirty years.

A debate between two kinds of individualism, reductive behaviorism and dualistic Cartesianism, continued to preoccupy both psychology and philosophy instead. Individualism, taking the situation of "self-confronting world" to be primary, was also central for opponents of behaviorism. If the self's experiences after birth are insufficient for accounting for matured social skills, then there must be innate cognitive structures doing the real work all along.

Noam Chomsky accordingly proposed that infants are born with something akin to an adult theory of mind consisting of basic structures of social cognition, especially a universal grammar for semantic interpretation to permit fast language acquisition. Jerry Fodor agrees, finding that the possession of an innate computational theory of mind is needed to explain the development of social skills during young childhood.[8]

John Searle's prominent attempts at social ontology and explaining social facts and institutions also harbored lingering Cartesianism. His internalism has never been disguised: "The brain is all we have for the purpose of representing the world to ourselves and everything we can use must be inside the brain." His further expression of this mental individualism states, "Collective mental phenomena of the sort we get in organized societies are themselves dependent on and derived from the mental phenomena of individuals."[9]

According to Searle, the most important kind of mental phenomena are internal symbolic representations. Since an individual cannot directly display his symbolic representations, he uses language to express them, and that behavioral conduct is observed by others, so that they can theoretically infer what symbols are intended. On Searle's account, our capacity to see the match between someone else's representations and our own permits what he called "collective intentionality": two or more people who happen to intend the same thing. However, Searle's individualism remains strict: "All human intentionality exists only in individual human brains."[10]

Searle's brains can speak at each other, but that can't speak with one voice. Since group plans depend on shared commitments, and one's commitments are in the form of symbolic representations requiring linguistic expression, then one can only tell whether another person has the same commitment through attending to that person's statements. However, not just any sort of statements will do. I can form a theory of your mental commitments, according to Searle, only after you utter "declarations" that state your intentions. Searle rightly denies that "We-intentions" are reducible without meaningful remainder down to sets of "I-intentions." However, his Cartesian Theory of Mind assumptions obstruct any explanation of how "We-intentions" could first form or ever find each other.

Cartesian individualism obstructs practical collective intentionality. I could learn that "You intend activity A" and match that up with "I intend A," but so far, all that adds up to is "Both you and I intend A," not "We intend to do A together in a particular way now." How do children begin to participate in collective intentionality? Searle's Cartesianism assumes far too much.

What if one of us is immature and unskilled, unsure about how we could do activity A? If I have little idea how we could do A, can I really intend that "We do A" in just the same way as another intends to do A, even if I want to do A and I understand that you intend doing A? "We-intentions," however vague, must be developmentally and situationally prior to "I-intentions." A small child can intend to "help father bake a cake" in some vague way because the child anticipates cake, but the child and the father are not sharing the same idea "I want us to bake a cake." Only the joint intention that "We will bake a cake" initiates and coordinates their particular "I" intentions during the baking.

Developmentally, there is a vast practical gap between "We intend activity A" and "We are doing A." During young childhood, none of us began engaging in any sort of group activity by first conceiving what we are supposed to do, verifying that all of us intend to do this together by listening to each other's utterances, and then undertaking our specific conduct to complete the group activity. Familiar customs among adults look that way, but intentionality could not be like that for early humans lacking sentential language or today's young initiates lacking experience.

A broad definition of social cognition is needed, such as: "Social cognition, more generally, constitutes the process by which people think about and make sense of other people, themselves, and social situations."[11] This view locates it within its proper home of situations containing people conducting practices and modifying their habitats. Expansive depictions of social cognition's core role in explaining human psychology, society, and culture, have become mainstream.[12]

Individual minds are not assembling society. Sociality is constructing individual minds. Investigations of "the social brain" have been underway in a variety of interrelated fields, from developmental and abnormal psychology to cognitive science and social neuroscience. There are robust empirical resources for understanding intentionality, intelligence, agency, and responsibility within the context of social cognition within communal and cultural groups.[13]

Social cognition cannot be an emergent phenomenon from aggregate individual cognitions. Any individualizable cognitions, including much of self-consciousness and agency, are emergent from a more fundamental field of embodied and dynamic social interaction.

Eliot R. Smith and Frederica Conrey summarize this research trend:

(a) Cognition is for the adaptive regulation of action, and mental representations are action oriented.

(b) Cognition is embodied, both constrained and facilitated by our sensorimotor abilities as well as our brains. (c) Cognition and action are situated in the sense of being contingent on specific aspects of the agent's social environment. (d) Cognition is distributed across brains and the environment and across social agents (e.g., when information is discussed and evaluated in groups).[14]

Once taken to be exclusive possessions of minds taken singly, our complex cognitive processes are proving to be capacities only of brains taken communally and thinking distributively.[15]

Pragmatism takes the most radical view: comprehending anything involves social cognition. Navigating a grocery store from entrance to exit with purchases is a series of social cognition tasks, while choosing what one's children like to eat, justifying that expensive cut of meat, and paying at the check-out line. Remembering what others have done, recognizing what other people are doing, communicating with others, recalling what others think, collaborating in practices, and anticipating what others may do in the future, are tasks at the heart of whatever we are doing every minute of every day.

What could you possibly do, besides the physiological abilities of any mammal, where no other human being could be involved? Life as a human is to behave as a human and think as a human. You didn't invent that. Pervasive social cognition is not a specialized production out of individual thinking. All cognition consults and serves social cognition through life's innumerable activities and practices.

The theory of social cognition explains why we do not first develop internally aware minds and then inferentially project mental states on others. More generally, we do not infer internal mental states of others that have some separate ontological status from features of observable behaviors. What we observe from infancy to adulthood is simply mindful behaviors of both ourselves and others. Mentality and intentionality are fully exemplified in these behaviors, or they are nowhere.

There is a logical point to admit, that a person's observably mindful behaviors underdetermine any estimate of that person's ongoing mental states. Yet this point is powerless to show that we must go far beyond information-poor behaviors to hypothesize information-rich mental entities. That behavioral underdetermination only shows how our thoughts about attitudes, intentions, and beliefs of us all, not excepting each of us ourselves, are somewhat vague and fallible judgments. There is never any need for anyone to postulate such things in a manner transcending all behaviors (and any neural events as well).

Group Intentions

Not only must humans learn how to engage in group activities before they have any adequate conception of what each of them is supposed to do, humans must engage in group activities before forming any ideas about any minds whatsoever, their own or others. Self-awareness gradually accumulates through attentiveness to what others are attempting. Only by successfully engaging in many sorts of group activities can young humans be acquiring minds.

The younger mind need not first form ideas about what an older mind intends before participating too, however haltingly and inadequately. Quite the opposite: only by attending to what the mature mind is doing and accomplishing, does the learning mind acquire some partial idea of the mature mind's intentions and beliefs. In effect, "We are doing activity A together" must developmentally come prior to "You are intending that we do A," which in turn is developmentally prior to "I intend that we do A"—and only after that does the child go on to form additional notions such as "I believe A should be done" or "I believe that A is done this way."

As the complexity of social activities increases, interconnections throughout the prefrontal cortex develop further, through infancy and childhood to early adulthood. The possession of human mentality consists of advanced capacities for focused, flexible, and successful social practices. Executive control over one's tasks and managing interpersonal relationships are two perspectives on the capacities for competency with human life.

Children acquire facility with the intentions, practices, and attitudes of others through social interaction. To ask the question, "When does the child leap from observations of mindful behavior to inferences about the inner mental states of others?" is a crucial misstep. To presuppose that one's appreciation for another's inner mental life is a matter separable from the appreciation for another's mindful conduct, is to assume that Theory of Mind is not merely distinguishable, but quite separable, from social conduct. This is a demonstrably inadequate view.

There is ample experimental support to disprove the presumption that knowledge of any mind, of one's own mind or minds of others, is developmentally prior to, or independent of, attentive participation in joint activities.[16] There is that classic example of infants passing the "False Belief" test, able to understand how others can have false beliefs. This is an important stage, always developing due to the wider context of an infant's enlarging ability to anticipate in the practical goals of others by observing their conduct. Estimating the false beliefs of others especially depends on the child perceiving what others can see and do. Reasoning to judgments about others' true beliefs develops at a later age.

Judging the intentions of others is rooted in a situational context. For example, a young child's development of executive control is another kind of practical functioning that grows right together with that child's practical ability to appreciate others' mental processes, such as attitudes, emotions, or beliefs. Developing executive functioning through group participation has priority. Training in executive function enhances both executive function and theory of mind, but training in theory of mind alone does not enhance either executive function or theory of mind.

Situational role-playing is crucial for normal cognitive development. Three-year-olds not only follow the intentions of others to engage in play but they figure out normative rules for conducting pretend play, and they enforce rules of play only on those who have willingly entered the field of pretense as actors. Games involving co-players sharing common goals are particularly efficient at enhancing executive and emotional control.[17]

The heavy reliance on social cognition for the development of one's cognitive capacities is not a temporary matter that diminishes in adulthood. What is adulthood, besides one's participation in multiple role-playing positions? Common processes underlie theory of mind capacity and participation with coordinated joint action in adulthood, and the brain's tendency to prioritize and preserve the impact of social interaction and coordination remains a pervasive adult phenomenon.

Cognition is what brains do, and as brains cognize jointly, then intentionality and agency operate in multiple brains properly functioning together, not in any aggregate of separate brains contingently acting side by side. Intentionality is basically *attentionality*. This is why each of the pragmatists, from Peirce and James to Dewey and Mead, took social experience to be as real as subjective experience.

This experiential sociality is no more mysterious than dancing, talking, or reading. From a linguistic perspective, symbolic communication must be about the fused responses of multiple organisms intentionally aware of their commonality. Pointing to brains generating experience only makes social experience more plausible. From a neurological perspective, why should the Hebbian process (introduced by Donald Hebb in 1949) of "neurons firing together are wiring together" halt at skull or skin? Brains learning together are literally developing together.

Socialization *is* signification *is* habituation. Higher-level cognitions involved with deliberate practices require simultaneous and synchronized operations across multiple brains that have grown together through shared experiences, intentions, communications, and practices. Synchronies of mentality and harmonies of society reflect each other. People can do many things by themselves, but only because they grew up doing so much with others. Localizing the "real" cognition and the "genuine" agency within brains taken singly must be false to both the natural development of brains and the social psychology of cognition.

Collaborative Thinking

The development of social cognition, only sketched in this chapter, constitutes the solution, or rather the dissolution, of the philosophical problem of other minds. Searle and so many other philosophers and psychologists have had it backwards. The mentality of individuals develops from, and operates with, the group mentality of organized societies.

Neither "inner" consciousness, "innate" concepts, "private" intentions, "a priori" truths, "pure" essences, nor "qualia" phenomena, or further examples of permanence's fictions, can keep the mind in splendid isolation. Not even thinking in itself. "Only I know the idea that I'm thinking" no more divides your mind from society than "Only I paint the picture that I'm painting" proves that no others had anything to do with art. You didn't invent thinking, or art. Or anything else you learned to make you human, including the ideas of selfhood and humanity. As Peirce argues,

... a person is not absolutely an individual. His thoughts are what he is "saying to himself," that is, saying to that other self that is just coming into life in the flow of time. When one reasons, it is that critical self that one is trying to persuade; and all thought whatsoever is a sign, and is mostly of the nature of language. The second thing to remember is that the man's circle of society (however widely or narrowly this phrase may be understood), is a sort of loosely compacted person, in some respects of higher rank than the person of an individual organism.[18]

Personhood has a broader ontological status than a "self." The natural telos of a human being is to become a person among persons in that communion called humanity.

The dynamics of group intentionality and agency deserve close study by many disciplines from history, sociology, and anthropology to economics and politics. It does remain a controversial philosophical topic. That is to be expected. Ordinary language, folk psychology, and Cartesian individualism conspire in the West to lend presumptive credibility for subjective intentions, individualized agency, and a revulsion towards "group mind" and "collective society."

Philosophy had not forgotten how absolute idealism, or any transpersonal collectivism, threatened the effective autonomy of individual persons.[19] What would a person's own plans and deeds be, if the absolute (or the general will, and so on) is already thinking what can be properly thought? Allowing a social mind to cause and control how we think, or how we behave, could hardly seem to be an improvement on absolutism, and a fast road towards totalitarianism.

Oddly, philosophers safely naturalizing and individualizing the mind by reducing free will to underpinning neural states are able to turn in repugnance against the notion of a collective mind overriding personal responsibility. Even more ironically, while modern philosophy disdains any long-past evolutionary basis to collective responsibility, it praises ethical rules to constrain the conduct of organizations motivated by individualistic ideologies and theologies of recent invention. In any case, hypocrisy aside, both absolutism and reductivism forget the ontological option of systemic holism.

Neither agency nor responsibility is at any risk from a socially *distributed* theory of mentality and agency. First and foremost, each contributes just as much talent as one wants, and accordingly receives as much empowerment as the group enables. Furthermore, one's capacity for effective productivity is immeasurably greater within society than whatever one could ever think or do on one's own. Finally, taking the social nature of cognition seriously, one's enculturation into adult roles powerfully molds both one's modes of agency and one's self-conception of one's own agency.

Consciousness and conscientiousness are on the same range of social experience from the most personal to the most collective. Just as physicality and mentality are just modes of dynamic reality characterized by function, subjectivity and objectivity are modes of mentality distinguishable by intent.

Accounts of group or collective intentionality are taking advantage of experimental psychology and neuroscience.[20] Because participation in shared practices with common goals is so tightly interfused with individual goal pursuit, individual intentions and personal agency cannot be neatly distinguished when studying interpersonal synchronous conduct. All the same, no one feels irresponsible or robotic while singing in a chorus or cooking a meal together, and everything about the brain's social cognition would prevent one from feeling that way. What I am trying to do is part of what we are doing, because we are doing it together while we intend the same outcome.

We share responsibility for success and failure, unless a joint agreement about particular individual responsibility can assign one or another more credit or blame. No matter the results, each of us remains responsible for choosing how to join efforts and apportion outcomes. To enjoy complete responsibility from start to finish, just do it all yourself and try to enjoy the meager fruits. Responsibility is worth little while humans are still pounding rocks and fleeing predators.

Summary

Pragmatism regards intentional and responsible agency as enlargeable facilities for living, not as simple "on or off" properties for mind. Control over choice is a relatively simple ability, inherent to any appreciable nervous system. Thinking about what might get chosen for which goal is vastly more complex and significant. Larger brain size yields control over a greater range of activities, while brains evolved for joint collaboration such as ours produce control over innumerable opportunities.

Freely participating in accomplishing more is the only freedom worth having for persons. Causality and sociality are enabling conditions, not obstructions, for autonomous agents acquiring ever-greater efficacious capabilities. There is no point to philosophy's quest to protect autonomy or rationality from nature's ways. Humanity is not what it once was. So long as sociality grows more intelligent, responsible freedom grows too.[21] That co-development of humanity's possibilities and practices has a name: Culture.

CULTURE AND PERSON

Persons are selves crafted from culture, not directly from biology. Personhood is far more than molecular or metabolic, but concluding that persons must be unnatural is too hasty. If biology evolved crafty humans, and then they developed societies, which educate selves into persons, that journey reconciles nature with personhood. Persons are no more unnatural than peacocks or pastries. Humanity happens to specialize in personhood.

Persons, complete with artful skills and responsible agency, are cultural achievements. They couldn't spring from just anywhere. Persons can create other persons, just as minds form more minds. The organic nature to mindful selves and responsible persons is what situates humanity within naturality.

In many ways, personhood is humanity's ultimate art form. Persons are special because they evolved with humanity itself, the source of everything we can be. Pragmatism finds that everything about minds, selves, and persons is congruent with our encultured existence as organic beings in this earthly world. Pragmatism completes its naturalistic worldview with this philosophical anthropology.

Biocultural Co-evolution

Staging culture within nature may pose special difficulties that tempt unnatural solutions if nature is regarded as just mechanistic or culture is viewed as only conventional. Nature's blunt forces don't look like plausible causes for norms of rationality or morality. Society's artificed ways do not seem responsible for them either. Is there a third option? Having made the first mistake in asking nature *or* society to be responsible for what we know and value, the next mistake is a leap *beyond* them, assigning responsibility to some unnatural (platonic, spiritual, theistic, etc.) origin instead. False dilemmas abound.

A better understanding of humanity's origins gives large credit to the biocultural co-evolution of humanity. Anthropologist Joseph Henrich outlines this process:

> . . . natural selection favored genes for building brains with abilities to learn from others. These learning

abilities, when operating in populations and over time, can give rise to subtly adaptive behavioral repertoires, including those related to fancy tools and large bodies of knowledge about plants and animals. These emergent products arose initially as unintended consequences of the interaction of learning minds in populations, over time.[1]

We humans have been made to think as we can, not by blind evolution alone, or bright invention alone, but through their long-entangled co-creations.[2] As our *Homo* line branched farther away from great apes, evolutionary pressures began to develop super-learners, acquiring clever behaviors from social cues and cares. From infancy, simple capacities easily engage with promptings from one's elders, to guide strengthening habits, then prepare the child for further role-taking in collaborations, and so on. Learning itself has to be learned, but this is no paradox. Childhood evolved.[3]

Babies arrived with propensities to learn so quickly that spastic motions soon become proclivities during childhood, and maturing skills can promptly be taught to others. Social mentality gradually became more heritable than selfish egoism. *Homo* ancestors, particularly *Homo habilis* and *Homo erectus*, accelerated this self-perpetuating and enlarging cycle, driving larger brain sizes, prolonged juvenile traits, and complex interpersonal relations, which in turn allowed for craftier invention and knowledge retention.

Most importantly, intentionality was increasingly recursive as memory expanded. That development allowed group coordination for participatory practices such as dancing, singing, mimetic (guttural and gestural) language, shared childrearing, instruction, and reciprocal morality. Those original cultural forms in turn permitted more effective tool-use, strategic hunting, food processing, security, and solidarity.[4]

Partly genetic and partly conventional, what proved necessary for the survival of both individuals and groups (that distinction blurring in the super-social *Homo* species) then became essential for trained mentality. That pseudo-debate over whether "gene selection," "individual selection," or "group selection" has driven hominin evolution over millions of years is a relic of needless reductionism. Very little at one level was ever altering independently from the other levels, and modifications were happening for many of the same reasons. Given opportunities for concerted attentiveness, distant ancestors evolved as they discovered practices conducive to better survival together.

Reductionism is particularly heedless when accounting for the communal workings of symbolism. The initial sorts of symbolism were not inscribed materially, nor inspired mentally, but embodied in others' stylized and expressive actions. To reverse a theological turn of phrase, in our own dwelling, Flesh became Word. After participatory synchrony was established, role-taking and rites in miniature provide the intelligible structure for the rest of our invented normative practices. When an infant happily claps along in rhythm with others, the rest of culture is details.

No magical leap from animal-like signals to articulate sentences ever happened. It took four or five million years and a flexible prefrontal cortex for intentionality to rise from the second-order stage (awareness that others have their beliefs) to the third-order (communicating one's own belief to change another's) and then fourth-order (communicating beliefs to be entertained by multiple hearers).[5] Fourth-order intentionality allows for role-taking within normative practices with the awareness that others appreciate one's own participatory role. This is the emergence of socializing, and hence the self.

As a founding sociologist, former student of Dewey, and admirer of James, Charles Horton Cooley pragmatically described the nature of the personal self with his metaphor of the "looking-glass self." Summarized neatly, "I am not what I think I am and I am not what you think I am; I am what I think that you think I am."[6] This fourth-order intentionality supplies the cognitive grounding for both attentive personhood and normative practice. They are the same thing from two perspectives, internally and externally.

This social intentionality of the personal self predates *Homo sapiens*. Late *Homo erectus* branches to *heidelbergensis* and then *neanderthalensis* apparently applied it. Their practices, such as toolmaking from multiple precise steps, multi-stage food preparation, and fair third-party punishment, for example, are capabilities practically impossible to acquire from imitation alone. A large neocortex, larger group sizes, social symbolism, and complex intentionality was involved. Fully grammatical speech with a large vocabulary arrived later, and its syntax recursivity, a useful sophistication, just tracked the earlier recursivity of intentionality.

The great cultural revolution occurred, not when *Homo sapiens* at last could start discussing their domiciles, sharper blades, rock paintings, and jewelry around 100,000 years ago, but much earlier, when previous *Homo* species were forging what was to be culture around 800–400 thousand years ago. Human universals descend from that first inheritance, while particular cultures sprang from the second. Other generic traits and behaviors are deeper inheritances from *Ardipithecus ramidus* and *Australopithecus* on to *H. habilis*.

New fields for cognitive archaeology and paleoanthropology are investigating the prolonged biocultural evolution of teamwork, teaching, technology, musicality, language, and artistry.[7] These fields are converging on a view of *Homo* development and humanity's inheritance that was suggested by the functionalism of classical pragmatism and endorsed by contemporary pragmatists.

On pragmatism's account of norms for thought, what society trains into a new mind had earlier been a novelty preserved by practical advantage. A new mind's formation through training, facilitated by a brain evolutionarily prepared for that learning, results in neural linkages and patterns so strongly channeled that resulting thought patterns and behaviors feel innate and inescapable. That conversion of novelty to inevitability through neurology would seem paradoxical except for millions of years of bio-cultural co-evolution. Enculturation succeeds. As Dewey stated, "The acquired may moreover become so deeply ingrained as to be for all intents and purposes native, a fact recognized in the common saying that 'habit is second nature.'"[8]

Our cultural forms, encompassing everything learnable, replicable, thinkable, and teachable, became humanity's nature, as our "second nature." Learning, playing, and teaching were our first cultural practices, and all else followed, including personhood.[9]

Cultural Performance

Encultured cognition, having reached higher orders of intentionality, can now achieve introspective contemplation,

A new mind's formation through training, facilitated by a brain evolutionarily prepared for that learning, results in neural linkages and patterns so strongly channeled that resulting thought patterns and behaviors feel utterly innate and inescapable.

perceptive observation, perspectival depiction, and narrative fiction. Other philosophies take these capacities as evidence for such notions as unworldly essences, sense data, inner representations, and possible worlds. Pragmatism cannot deny that imaginative people can focus on seeming fixities, and such matters do have cognitive utility as proxies. However, culture still accounts for the richest cognitive processes. Sophisticated symbolic capacities of human intelligence are scaffolded on the extended mind of linguistic sociality, offloading cognitive work onto the manipulation of external symbols.[10]

The invention of symbolism, followed by gesticulation, speech, and writing, takes advantage of the way that cognition specializes in dealing with our transactions with deliberately modified features of our environs. Human intelligence can offload cognitive work onto that symbolic field around us so that it retains or even manipulates information for us, and we harvest that information on a need-to-know basis. That makes the modified environment part of the socially cognitive system. The information flow between minds/brains and objects is so dense and continuous that, for scientists studying cognitive activity, the lone thinker is not a sufficiently meaningful unit of analysis. The production of higher cognitive activity does not come from mind or brain alone, but instead blends the functionalities of mind/brain and its crafted habitat.

These core views of pragmatism, in conjunction with embodied, enactive, and extended (non-representational) cognitive science, resolve perennial puzzles about the mind–body relation, the naturality of sophisticated cognitive operations, and the cultural origin of creative reasoning. For our human cognition, the most important part of the lived environment needing management is the social world: humans exchanging information and collaboration. We never represent the same thing twice, for it's not the same encounter and we are not the same observer. The brain's deeply networked architectures are not about processing "representations," but more about "re-performatives" as elements of adroit and appropriate behavior.[11] For humans, our experience is thoroughly social and cultural. Cognizing with adeptness is accomplished through transmitted modes of cultural activities engaging our brains.

The most sophisticated modes of human cognition are assemblages and refinements of lower-level cognitive processes. These complex modes of thought, seemingly far from mere matter or biology, remain embodied and functional for practical success. Higher self-conscious thinking—such as reflection, inference, and hypothesizing—are socially invented and instructed capacities to attentively focus on ways to generalize practical habits for flexible applications. These higher social capacities serve to coordinate group cooperative practices where much collective creativity is needed to maintain efficiency in the face of shifting environing conditions.

Enlarging imagination and working memory grow a contemplative space where techniques can be experimentally rehearsed and attempted on analogous new problems. Even pure imagination, conceptual play, and aesthetic contemplation are creative capacities existing to refine practice, even though we can also do them in isolation from practical concerns. These creative modes permitted, among other things, the fixation of concepts and relations among concepts, leading to explicit credible inference.

Sophisticated kinds of rational thinking—particularly methodical reasonings and experimental methods—are refined developments from integrating cognitive processes. The most veritable knowledge that humanity can acquire from logic and science are products of these culturally designed and educationally transmitted techniques. The reason why scientific hypotheses should be understood realistically is because scientific communities can elicit reliable transactions with theorized entities.[12]

Scientific knowledge is continuous with practical and technological skill. Much of human experience, most of morality, and all of knowledge is an emergent feature of socially epistemic practices. All a priori, conceptual, and linguistic truths are internal to one or another epistemic practice. Because no a priori conceptual rigidity can dictate terms of empirical adequacy, only the practical adequacy of a knowledge system is relevant to its overall validity. By avoiding epistemic dualism and reductivist monism, both epistemology and ethics are (holistically) naturalized, fitting them into the natural world of encultured humans. Nothing spiritual, transcendental, or supernatural is needed to account for mind.

Complex modes of human cognition aim at social competence, technological expertise, and knowledge of reality. Culture educates members of society into various forms of responsible intelligence, and expects their dutiful use for group goals, so they ultimately answer to pragmatic criteria of success. With us *sapiens*, "humanity" consists of central cultural praxes, primarily artwork creation, tool machination, cohort education, linguistic narration, musical composition, expressive ritualization, spiritual rumination, moral indoctrination, sports competition, trade transaction, tribal coalition, and kinship cohesion.

Discursive and interpretive norms are intrinsically part of such practices and thus part of each of us as persons, rather than innately prior to them or descending transcendentally to structure them.[13] Our life as a "personal self" is bound up with cultural praxes, those "symbolic spheres" of participatory life. The "person" is an artifactual embodiment and expression of culture. Long-distant ancestors gradually created persons; nothing else in heaven or on earth could.

Reason, knowledge, and duty persist due to education and experimentation, and they are eventually answerable to practical justification within cultural contexts. There is no logic–practice dichotomy. Whatever seems certain and necessary is due to cognitive operations so habitually ingrained that easily trainable brains either implement them subconsciously or our thinking relies on them so thoroughly. But minds can be changed over time, across generations.

Advanced learning is capable of questioning, amending, or abandoning the firmest of beliefs through empirical inquiry and experimental science. Advanced philosophy, especially pragmatism's pluralistic naturalism, refutes worldviews that divorce mind from world, persons from practices, or culture from nature.

Summary

Cognition and culture are thoroughly natural. The evolution of the human species, with the biocultural co-evolution of complex human associations and practices, suffices to explain all features of cognition. The two modes of evolution are not disjunctive—no form of cognition is independent from either mode, although complex forms of human cognition are mainly cultural in origin and function.

We humans experience the world in ways prepared by sociality to engage a responsive nature. Our brains perform cognition in ways prepared by natural evolution to perpetuate society, which supplies all the practices of humanity.

Everything about humanity is embedded within ongoing reality. Continuities as well as contingencies are prevalent. Pragmatism's worldview offers these guiding tenets:

Reality is holistic: continuities are pervasive throughout all reality.

Ontology is dynamic: whatever has actuality is always changing and interactive.

Explanation is contextual: co-responsive conditions account for the course of processes.

Learning is creative: new information arises from imaginative and inventive explorations.

Knowledge is communal: improving knowledge requires collaborative experimentation.

Nature can be reasonable, because its energetic patterns can operate in systemically organized ways, allowing their metabolic formations of organisms. Reason can be natural, because its functional processes can work for embodied encultured humans, allowing their prolific avocations with nature. The cosmos hosts persons, who reflect their home while striving for fulfillment.

Everything that this naturalistic philosophy requires for its demonstration lies within its worldview, including the social intelligence and cultural techniques permitting its justifications. Pragmatism is a coherent, complete, and self-sufficient worldview.

ACKNOWLEDGMENTS

Some paragraphs of chapters 10 and 11 are adapted from passages in two previous publications. Franks, David D. and Jonathan H. Turner, eds., "Social Cognition and the Problem of Other Minds," in *Handbook of Neurosociology* (Berlin: Springer, 2012); and "Neuropragmatism and the Reconstruction of Scientific and Humanistic Worldviews," in *Neuroscience, Neurophilosophy and Pragmatism: Brains at Work with the World*, edited by Tibor Solymosi and John R. Shook (London: Palgrave Macmillan, 2014).

Absolutism
The metaphysical combination of Idealism and Monism. All reality consists of one ultimate Mind, including finite minds like ours and anything perceivable and knowable. It relies on epistemic or mystic Reductionism to depict anything that seems natural or material as either mentally dependent or unreal.

Behaviorism
The epistemological and scientific position that any mental and psychological activity, conscious or unconscious, eventually manifests in overt behaviors of agents. A strict version, that only behavioral matters (not anything mental) are appropriate objects of knowledge, supports Materialism.

Determinism
What is changeless needs little or no explanation, but any event of novelty and change must be caused by other event(s) coincident or precedent in time. Strict determinism, in opposition to Pluralism, says that an event necessarily occurs precisely in all its features due to prior cause(s) according to invariant laws.

Dualism
In metaphysics, two different kinds of reality are fundamental but independent and discontinuous. In epistemology, (mental) knowledge represents mind-independent realities unaffected by that knowing. Typical dualities are fact vs. value, matter vs. mind, creation vs. God, freedom vs. determinism, and so on.

Empiricism
The kind of epistemology claiming that all knowledge must be reasonably based, directly or indirectly, on observing and experimenting. All confirmation is empirical. Rationalism opposes Empiricism with something nonempirical, such as intuitive certainty or conceptual clarity, also needed for knowledge.

Epistemology
Constructs and compares theories about rational justifications required for any knowledge of truth. Epistemology includes views about origins of

information, criteria for assessing plausibility and validity, kinds of inferences warranting conclusions, and tactics for avoiding fallacies and falsehoods.

Fallibilism
Reliability and revisability are key features of knowledge, rather than strict necessity or permanent fixity. No knowledge is infallible, and much gets discarded as false, but sound methodologies yield improving and expanding knowledge over time.

Historicism
The Relativism view that knowledge (practical and theoretical) is communal and genealogical, expressing a unique and irreplaceable cultural heritage. In social theory, a culture's customs, institutions, arts, morals, politics, and so on, are only comprehended for their own sake within that culture's historical pathway.

Holism
Continuities and interrelationships prevail among all existences. Nothing is independent from context, and parts are best explained by wholes. Holism, like Monism, opposes Dualism, but non-monistic Holism can combine with Pluralism. In social theory, individuals are created and sustained within societies.

Idealism
The metaphysical view that only mind, its capabilities, and its constructs are ultimately real. Monistic idealism uses mentalistic Reductionism to justify Absolutism, while pluralistic idealism leads instead towards Subjectivism.

Individualism
In metaphysics, the view that particular individuals are just as real, or more real, than any other kind of reality. Individualism is compatible with Holism but lends itself to Subjectivism. In social theory, the view that society only exists due to, and for the sake of, individual members who bear higher value.

Materialism
The version of Naturalism asserting a Monism of inert and insensate physical reality. Materialism relies on scientific Reductionism to account for anything seeming immaterial ("phenomenal" or "mental" for example) as either

materially dependent or unreal. Pluralism is opposed to Materialism, while Determinism is allied.

Metaphysics
Ponders what all ontologies (and everything existing) have in common, and what is responsible for reality or is most real. Ranking one kind of reality as supreme or solely real inspires metaphysical Dualism, along with problems about part–whole relations, perceptual knowledge, mind–body connections, free will, and so on. Holism and Monism oppose Dualism.

Monism
The metaphysical view that there is only one kind of reality throughout all existences. Each sort of thing is a manifestation of, or essentially participates in, this unique reality. Monism is far more compatible with Holism than Pluralism. Typical monisms are Idealism and Materialism.

Naturalism
Nature is exclusively and ultimately real, and all explanations are empirical and appeal to something natural. Naturalism is realistic and non-dualistic, but it typically aligns with Pluralism to accommodate both mind and matter, body and spirit, and so on. The Reductionism version of naturalism is Materialism.

Ontology
What is taken to exist by some area of experience, practice, or inquiry. A discourse's terms, whether about a dream, a drama, a dogma, a discipline, or a database, is an ontology. Ontology is inherently pluralistic, unless overruled by scientific or metaphysical Reductionism.

Pluralism
Innumerable kinds of existences make up all of reality, having mostly contingent relations among them, so plenitude, discreteness, and diversity characterize all beings. Social pluralism opposes cultural uniformity by recognizing the value of different groups or the individuality of each person.

Pragmatism
A philosophical worldview that integrates Process philosophy and Pluralism with Holism, Fallibilism, and Naturalism. In social theory, Pragmatism emphasizes Historicism, the value of cultural diversity, and liberal democracy.

Process philosophy
In opposition to permanence philosophy, anything real is gradually changing both internally and relationally along with everything else. Respect for the universality of processes is aligned with Pluralism.

Rationalism
The kind of epistemology claiming that knowledge is reasonable due to a non-experiential basis, such as intuitive certainty or conceptual clarity, rather than experiential learning alone. A rationalist epistemology finding two spheres of knowledge, one mainly empirical and one principally rational, leads to Dualism.

Realism
In metaphysics, most of reality exists independently from mind, mental activity (such as consciousness or experience), and knowledge. In epistemology, objective truths are knowable about independent reality while minds attend it. Making knowledge more dependent on mind leads to Idealism or Subjectivism.

Reductionism
The scientific or metaphysical strategy of rationally explaining how one ontology is really just an aspect, function, property, component, etc. of another ontology. A failed explanation encourages ontological Pluralism or even Dualism.

Relativism
Truths are knowable within communities, each upholding their own criteria for credible knowledge. Knowledge from communities can be compared and even shared, but no community's knowledge has a rational basis to invalidate another's. In social theory, important values of communities and cultures are similarly distinctive and incommensurable.

Representationalism
In epistemology, valid knowledge must resemble or replicate relevant features or structures of what is known. An empiricist version expects observational and propositional knowledge to accurately represent what is known. In science, a realistic hypothesis can accurately model what it postulates.

Skepticism
Claims to know about fixed or final truths have no rational basis, so no truth exists, and doubt is more reasonable. Common sense or personal opinion must

serve for belief, and my "fact" can't prove your different "fact" false. Relativism and Fallibilism offer compromise alternatives to Skepticism.

Subjectivism

In metaphysics, the idealistic position that all reality consists only of individual minds and their interrelationships. In epistemology, the skeptical position that any belief or knowledge only has validity for the individual thinker. The greatest opposition to Subjectivism comes from Realism and Naturalism.

Voluntarism

In metaphysics, the position that every existence at every scale has dynamic potency and some degree of volition and purpose. In epistemology, the theory that all knowledge arises from, and only receives validity through, the willful and purposive activities of knowers.

NOTES

Chapter 1

1. Charles W. Morris, "Neo-Pragmatism and the Ways of Knowing," *The Monist* 38.4 (October 1928): 494–510. Also see: Alan R. Malachowski, *The New Pragmatism* (Montreal: McGill–Queen's University Press, 2010); Omayra Cruz, *Neo-Pragmatisms and New Romanticisms* (London and New York: Routledge, 2009); David Hildebrand, *Beyond Realism and Antirealism: John Dewey and the Neopragmatists* (Nashville: Vanderbilt University Press, 2003); Douglas McDermid, *The Varieties of Pragmatism: Truth, Realism, and Knowledge from James to Rorty* (London: Continuum, 2006); Cheryl Misak, ed., *New Pragmatists* (Oxford: Oxford University Press, 2007).

2. Comparative treatments of pragmatism include these works: A. J. Ayer, *The Origins of Pragmatism: Studies in the Philosophies of Charles Sanders Peirce and William James* (San Francisco: Freeman, Cooper, 1968); Arthur O. Lovejoy, *The Thirteen Pragmatisms and Other Essays* (Baltimore: Johns Hopkins University Press, 1968); Israel Scheffler, *Four Pragmatists: A Critical Introduction to Peirce, James, Mead, and Dewey* (New York: Humanities Press, 1974); H. O. Mounce, *The Two Pragmatisms: From Peirce to Rorty* (London and New York: Routledge, 1997); John P. Murphy, *Pragmatism From Peirce to Davidson* (Boulder, CO: Westview Press, 1990); Cheryl Misak, *The American Pragmatists* (Oxford: Oxford University Press, 2013).

3. James, William. *Works: Pragmatism*, 31. See Further Reading for explanations of citations to critical editions of the pragmatists.

4. An account of pragmatism's origins is told in Frank Ryan, Brian Butler, and James Good, ed., *The Real Metaphysical Club: The Philosophers, Their Debates, and Selected Writings from 1870 to 1885* (Albany: State University of New York Press, 2019).

5. James, *Works: Pragmatism*, 42.

6. James, *Works: Pragmatism*, 97, dashes and italics in the original.

7. Peirce, *CP* 5.555, c.1903.

8. William James to Henry James, May 4, 1907, in *The Letters of William James*, ed. Henry James (New York, 1920), vol. 2, 279.

9. Presidential addresses of the American Philosophical Association display such wide variety. See John R. Shook, ed., *Historical Essays in 20th Century American Philosophy* (Charlottesville, VA: Philosophy Documentation Center, 2015).

10. James T. Kloppenberg, *Uncertain Victory: Social Democracy and Progressivism in European and American Social Thought, 1870–1920* (New York: Oxford University Press, 1986); James Livingston, *Pragmatism and the Political Economy of Cultural Revolution, 1850–1940* (Chapel Hill, NC: University of North Carolina Press, 1994); Andrew Feffer, *The Chicago Pragmatists and American Progressivism* (Ithaca, NY: Cornell University Press, 1993); Morris Dickstein, ed., *The Revival of Pragmatism: New Essays on Social Thought, Law, and Culture* (Durham, NC: Duke University Press, 1998); John Pettegrew, ed., *A Pragmatist's Progress? Richard Rorty and American Intellectual History* (Lanham, MD: Rowman & Littlefield, 2000).

11. Consult the following works: Richard J. Bernstein, *Beyond Objectivism and Relativism: Science, Hermeneutics, and Praxis* (Philadelphia: University of Pennsylvania Press, 1983); W. J. T. Mitchell, ed., *Against Theory: Literary Studies and the New Pragmatism* (Chicago: University of Chicago Press, 1985); Chantal Mouffe, ed., *Deconstruction and Pragmatism: Critchley, Derrida, Laclau and Rorty* (London and New York: Routledge, 1996). Mike Sandbothe and William Egginton, eds., *The Pragmatic Turn in Philosophy: Contemporary Engagements Between Analytic and Continental Thought* (Albany: State University of New York Press, 2004); Paul Fairfield, ed., *John Dewey and Continental Philosophy* (Carbondale, IL: Southern Illinois University Press, 2010).

Chapter 2

1. Jeroen Bouterse and Bart Karstens, "A Diversity of Divisions: Tracing the History of the Demarcation between the Sciences and the Humanities," *Isis* 106.2 (June 2015): 341–352.

2. Robert J. Richards, *The Romantic Conception of Life: Science and Philosophy in the Age of Goethe* (Chicago: University of Chicago Press, 2010); Frederick Beiser, *The Fate of Reason: German Philosophy from Kant to Fichte* (Cambridge, MA: Harvard University Press, 2009).

3. Trevor Pearce, *Pragmatism's Evolution: Organism and Environment in American Philosophy* (Chicago: University of Chicago Press, 2020); John R. Shook, *Dewey's Empirical Theory of Knowledge and Reality* (Nashville: Vanderbilt University Press, 2000); Hans Joas and Daniel R. Huebner, eds., *The Timeliness of George Herbert Mead* (Chicago: University of Chicago Press, 2016).

4. Ian Hacking, *The Taming of Chance* (Cambridge, UK: Cambridge University Press, 1990).

5. Peirce, *EP* 1.300; *CP* 1.155; *EP* 1.331.

6. Kenneth L. Ketner and A. F. Stewart, "The Early History of Computer Design: Charles Sanders Peirce and Marquand's Logical Machines," *Princeton*

University Library Chronicle 45.3 (Spring 1984): 186–211; Risto Hilpinen, "Peirce's Logic," in *The Rise of Modern Logic From Leibniz to Frege*, eds. D. M. Gabbay and J. Woods (Amsterdam: Elsevier North-Holland, 2004), 611–658; Jaakko Hintikka, "The Place of C. S. Peirce in the History of Logical Theory," in *The Rule of Reason: The Philosophy of Charles Sanders Peirce*, eds. J. Brunning and P. Forster (Toronto: University of Toronto Press, 1996), 13–33.

7. Gérard Deledalle, *Charles S. Peirce's Philosophy of Signs* (Bloomington, IN: Indiana University Press, 2000); Thomas A. Sebeok, *Signs: An Introduction to Semiotics*, 2nd ed. (Toronto: University of Toronto Press, 2001); T. L. Short, *Peirce's Theory of Signs* (Cambridge, UK: Cambridge University Press, 2007); Tony Jappy, ed., *The Bloomsbury Companion to Contemporary Peircean Semiotics* (London: Bloomsbury, 2019).

8. Laura Moorhead, "Down the Rabbit Hole: Tracking the Humanizing Effect of John Dewey's Pragmatism on Norbert Wiener," in *IEEE Conference on Norbert Wiener in the 21st Century* (Piscataway, NJ: IEEE, 2014), 1–8.

9. Mark Johnson and George Lakoff, "Why Cognitive Linguistics Requires Embodied Realism," *Cognitive Linguistics* 13.3 (2002): 245–263; James Russell, *What is Language Development? Rationalist, Empiricist, and Pragmatist Approaches to the Acquisition of Syntax* (Oxford: Oxford University Press, 2004); David Boersema, *Pragmatism and Reference* (Cambridge, MA: MIT Press, 2009); Daniel Dor, Chris Knight, and Jerome Lewis, eds., *The Social Origins of Language* (Oxford: Oxford University Press, 2014); Ezequiel A. Di Paolo, Elena Clare Cuffari, and Hanne De Jaegher, *Linguistic Bodies: The Continuity between Life and Language* (Cambridge, MA: MIT Press, 2018).

10. Francisco J. Varela, Eleanor Rosch, and Evan Thompson, *The Embodied Mind: Cognitive Science and Human Experience* (Cambridge, MA: MIT Press, 1991); Jean Valsiner and Rene Van Der Veer, *The Social Mind: Construction of the Idea* (Cambridge, UK: Cambridge University Press, 2000); Harold Blumer, *Symbolic Interactionism* (Englewood Cliffs, NJ: Prentice-Hall, 1969); Anselm L. Strauss, *Continual Permutations of Action* (New York: Aldine de Gruyter, 1993); Radu Bogdan, *Our Own Minds: Sociocultural Grounds for Self-Consciousness* (Cambridge, MA: MIT Press, 2010); Marcello Barbieri, ed., *Introduction to Biosemiotics: The New Biological Synthesis* (Dordrecht, Netherlands: Springer, 2008).

11. Thomas Wynn, Karenleigh Overmann, and Lambros Malafouris, "4E Cognition in the Lower Palaeolithic," *Adaptive Behavior* 29.2 (2021): 99–106; Walter J. Freeman, *How Brains Make Up Their Minds* (New York: Columbia University Press, 2001); Fausto Caruana and Italo Testa, eds., *Habits: Pragmatist*

Approaches from Cognitive Science, Neuroscience, and Social Theory (Cambridge, UK: Cambridge University Press, 2020).

12. David L. Leary, *The Routledge Guidebook to James's Principles of Psychology* (New York and London: Routledge, 2018).

13. Edward S. Reed, *James J. Gibson and the Psychology of Perception* (New Haven, CT: Yale University Press, 1988); Harry Heft, *Ecological Psychology in Context: James Gibson, Roger Barker, and the Legacy of William James's Radical Empiricism* (Mahwah, NJ: Lawrence Erlbaum Associates, 2001).

14. Francesca Michelini and Kristian Köchy, eds., *Jakob von Uexküll and Philosophy: Life, Environments, Anthropology* (New York and London: Routledge, 2020); Richard Lewontin and Richard Levins, *The Dialectical Biologist* (Cambridge, MA: Harvard University Press, 1985); Gregory Bateson, *Steps to an Ecology of Mind* (Chicago: University of Chicago Press, 1972).

15. Dewey, *How We Think*, MW 6: 265.

16. Alva Noë, *Out of Our Heads: Why You Are Not Your Brain, and Other Lessons from the Biology of Consciousness* (New York: Hill and Wang, 2009); Andy Clark, *Supersizing the Mind: Embodiment, Action, and Cognitive Extension* (New York: Oxford University Press, 2008); Daniel C. Dennett, *Kinds of Minds: Toward an Understanding of Consciousness* (New York: Basic Books, 1996); Evan Thompson, *Mind in Life: Biology, Phenomenology, and the Sciences of Mind* (Cambridge, MA: Harvard University Press, 2007); Tim Ingold, *The Perception of the Environment: Essays on Livelihood, Dwelling and Skill* (New York and London: Routledge, 2000); Mark Rowlands, *The New Science of the Mind: From Extended Mind to Embodied Phenomenology* (Cambridge MA: MIT Press, 2010); John R. Shook and Tibor Solymosi, eds., *Neuroscience, Neurophilosophy, and Pragmatism: Brains at Work with the World* (London: Palgrave Macmillan, 2014); Anthony Chemero, *Radical Embodied Cognitive Science* (Cambridge, MA: MIT Press, 2009); Pentti Määttänen, *Mind in Action: Experience and Embodied Cognition in Pragmatism* (Cham, Switzerland: Springer, 2018).

Chapter 3

1. Peirce, "The Architecture of Theories" *EP* 1: 288.

2. James, *Works: Pragmatism*, 78–79.

3. Dewey, "Time and Individuality" *ED* 1: 224.

4. Parallels and proximities with pragmatism can be ample. Randall E. Auxier, *Time, Will, and Purpose: Living Ideas from the Philosophy of Josiah Royce* (Chicago: Open Court, 2013); Mark Okrent, *Heidegger's Pragmatism: Understanding, Being, and the Critique of Metaphysics* (Ithaca, NY: Cornell University Press, 1988); Brian G. Henning, William T. Myers, and Joseph D. John, eds., *Thinking*

with *Whitehead and the American Pragmatists: Experience and Reality* (Lanham, MD: Lexington Books, 2015); Henry S. Levinson, *Santayana, Pragmatism, and the Spiritual Life* (Chapel Hill, NC: University of North Carolina Press, 1992).

5. Nietzsche's thought can be fairly co-extensive with pragmatism. See Pietro Gori, *Nietzsche's Pragmatism: Essays on Perspectival Thought* (Berlin: De Gruyter, 2019); and Manuel Dries and P. J. E. Kail, eds., *Nietzsche on Mind and Nature* (Oxford: Oxford University Press, 2015). On Bergson and Deleuze, see Simone Bignall, Sean Bowden, and Paul Patton, eds., *Deleuze and Pragmatism* (London and New York: Routledge, 2014). On existentialism, see also Christina Howells, *Sartre: The Necessity of Freedom* (Cambridge, UK: Cambridge University Press, 2009). Wilhelm Dilthey approaches Dewey's historicist naturalism.

6. Dewey, *Quest for Certainty, LW* 4: 13–14.

7. Joseph Margolis, *Pragmatism Without Foundations: Reconciling Realism and Relativism*, 2nd ed. (London: Continuum, 2007).

8. A pragmatist reconstruction of Kant and Hegel is Kenneth R. Westphal, *Grounds of Pragmatic Realism: Hegel's Internal Critique and Reconstruction of Kant's Critical Philosophy* (Leiden, Netherlands: Brill, 2017). On Quine, see Murray Murphey, *The Development of Quine's Philosophy* (Dordrecht, Netherlands: Springer, 2012).

9. Gabriele Gava and Robert Stern, eds., *Pragmatism, Kant, and Transcendental Philosophy* (London and New York: Routledge, 2016).

Chapter 4

1. James, *Works: Pragmatism*, 143.

2. Russell, *A History of Western Philosophy* (London: Allen and Unwin, 1946), 846.

3. Albert Einstein, "Foreword" in Phillip Frank, *Relativity* (Boston: Beacon Press, 1950), viii.

4. James, *Works: The Meaning of Truth*, 40–41.

5. W. V. Quine's "indispensability argument" argues that science's formulaic successes supply warrant for the real existence of mathematical entities too: "On What There Is," repr. in *From a Logical Point of View*, 2nd ed. (Cambridge, MA: Harvard University Press, 1980), 1–19; On pragmatism's view, the purity of mathematics maintains its unreality in guaranteeing its truths; there is no naturalistic or Platonic realism destined for mathematics. Consult Philip Kitcher, *The Nature of Mathematical Knowledge* (Oxford: Oxford University Press, 1984); and George Lakoff and Rafael E. Nuñez, *Where Mathematics Comes From: How the Embodied Mind Brings Mathematics Into Being* (New York: Basic Books, 2000).

6. Dewey judged that quantum mechanics was interpretable along the lines of his pragmatism. See Thomas C. Dalton, *Becoming John Dewey: Dilemmas of a Philosopher and Naturalist* (Bloomington, IN: Indiana University Press, 2002), chap. 7. Physicist Richard Healey concurs with pragmatism in *The Quantum Revolution in Philosophy* (Oxford: Oxford University Press, 2017).

7. Joshua Gert, *Primitive Colors: A Case Study in Neo-pragmatist Metaphysics and Philosophy of Perception* (Oxford: Oxford University Press, 2017); Mazviita Chirimuuta, *Outside Color: Perceptual Science and the Puzzle of Color in Philosophy* (Cambridge, MA: MIT Press, 2015).

8. Dewey, *LW* 1: 65.

9. Huw Price, "Causal Perspectivalism," in *Causation, Physics, and the Constitution of Reality: Russell's Republic Revisited*, eds. H. Price and R. Corry (Oxford: Oxford University Press, 2007), 250–292.

10. As argued by Nancy Cartwright, *The Dappled World: A Study of the Boundaries of Science* (Cambridge, UK: Cambridge University Press, 1999).

11. Peirce, *CP* 5.503.

12. Peirce, *CP* 5.431.

13. Peirce, *CP* 6.485.

Chapter 5

1. James, *Works: Pragmatism*, 96.

2. James, *Works: Pragmatism*, 38, emphases in original.

3. Wilfrid Sellars exemplifies the struggle to reconcile materialist empiricism with conceptual rationalism. See Willem A. deVries, *Wilfrid Sellars* (Chesham, UK: Acumen, 2005); and Robert Brandom, *From Empiricism to Expressivism: Brandom Reads Sellars* (Cambridge, MA: Harvard University Press, 2015).

4. Robert B. Brandom, *Perspectives on Pragmatism: Classical, Recent, and Contemporary* (Cambridge, MA: Harvard University Press, 2011), 22.

5. Due attention to entwinements of language, reason, and experience tends to send philosophers in pragmatist directions. See, for example, Richard Rorty's introduction and retrospective essays in *The Linguistic Turn*, 2nd ed. (Chicago: University of Chicago Press, 1992). Further examples multiplied, for example: Daniel Dennett, *The Intentional Stance* (Cambridge, MA: MIT Press, 1987); Donald Davidson, *The Essential Davidson* (Oxford: Oxford University Press, 2006); Robert Brandom, *Making It Explicit: Reasoning, Representing, and Discursive Commitment* (Cambridge, MA: Harvard University Press, 1994); John McDowell, *Mind and World* (Cambridge, MA: Harvard University Press, 1996); Fred Dretske, *Perception, Knowledge and Belief* (Cambridge, UK:

Cambridge University Press, 2000); Ruth Millikan, *Varieties of Meaning* (Cambridge, MA: MIT Press, 2004); Huw Price, *Expressivism, Pragmatism and Representationalism* (Cambridge, UK: Cambridge University Press, 2013).

6. In illustration, see Paul Boghossian and Timothy Williamson, *Debating the A Priori* (Oxford: Oxford University Press, 2020).

7. Peirce, *CP* 5.402.

8. James, *Works: Pragmatism*, 29.

9. Peirce, *EP* 2: 332.

10. James, *Works: Pragmatism*, 96–97.

11. Kenneth R. Westphal, *Grounds of Pragmatic Realism: Hegel's Internal Critique & Transformation of Kant's Critical Philosophy* (Leiden, Netherlands: Brill, 2018).

12. Dewey, *MW* 4: 68–69.

Chapter 6

1. A twentieth century exemplar is Bertrand Russell, *An Inquiry into Meaning and Truth* (London: George Allen and Unwin, 1940).

2. The subjectivism flourishing during the nineteenth and twentieth centuries is called Personalism. Jan Olof Bengtsson, *The Worldview of Personalism* (Oxford: Oxford University Press, 2006); Juan Manuel Burgos, *An Introduction to Personalism* (Washington, DC: Catholic University of America Press, 2018).

3. On modern absolutism, see William Sweet, ed., *Bernard Bosanquet and the Legacy of British Idealism* (Toronto: University of Toronto Press, 2007).

4. Much of non-theistic Buddhism can overlap with pragmatism. Steve Odin, *The Social Self in Zen and American Pragmatism* (Albany: State University of New York Press, 1996).

5. Peirce, *CP* 5.452. See also *CP* 5.525.

6. Dewey, *EW* 3: 66.

7. James, *Works: The Principles of Psychology*, vol. 1, 343–344.

8. James, *Works: The Meaning of Truth*, 45–46.

9. Dewey, *MW* 6: 447–448.

10. A recent defense of pragmatism from experience is Steven Levine, *Pragmatism, Objectivity, and Experience* (Cambridge, UK: Cambridge University Press, 2019).

11. Dewey, *ED* 1: 47–48.

12. My terminology of the "formulaic" and "concretic" proceeds from Dewey's distinction between universal and generic propositions in *Logic: The Theory of Inquiry*, *LW* 12: 263–279.

Chapter 7

1. Richard Rorty, *Objectivity, Relativism, and Truth* (Cambridge, UK: Cambridge University Press, 1991); Hilary Putnam, *The Threefold Cord: Mind, Body, and World* (New York: Columbia University Press, 1999); Nicholas Rescher, *Realism and Pragmatic Epistemology* (Pittsburgh: University of Pittsburgh Press, 2005); Richard J. Bernstein, *The Pragmatic Turn* (Malden, MA: Wiley-Blackwell, 2013).

2. Dewey, *The Quest for Certainty*, LW 4: 17, 18.

3. Dewey, *The Quest for Certainty*, LW 4: 23.

4. Dewey, *The Quest for Certainty*, LW 4: 140–141.

5. James, *Works: A Pluralistic Universe*, 99.

6. Peirce, *EP* 2: 129.

7. Royce, *The World and the Individual. First Series: The Four Historical Conceptions of Being* (New York: Macmillan, 1900), 112–132.

8. Dewey, *Essays in Experimental Logic*, MW 6: 111–122.

9. Edmund Gettier, "Is Justified True Belief Knowledge?" *Analysis* 23.6 (1963): 121–123.

10. See William Lycan, "The Gettier Problem Problem," in *Epistemology Futures*, ed. Stephen Hetherington (Oxford: Oxford University Press, 2006), 148–168; and John Turri, "In Gettier's Wake," in *Epistemology: The Key Thinkers*, ed. Stephen Hetherington (London: Continuum Press, 2012), 214–229.

11. See Roderick Chisholm, *The Problem of the Criterion* (Milwaukee.: Marquette University Press, 1973); and Richard Fumerton, "The Problem of the Criterion," in *The Oxford Handbook on Skepticism*, ed. John Greco (Oxford: Oxford University Press, 2008), 34–52.

Chapter 8

1. Christopher Hookway, "American Pragmatism: Fallibilism and Cognitive Progress" in *Epistemology: The Key Thinkers*, ed. Stephen Hetherington (London: Continuum, 2008), 153–171; Joseph Margolis, "Rethinking Peirce's Fallibilism," in Margolis, *Pragmatism Ascendent* (Stanford, CA: Stanford University Press, 2012), 51–110.

2. Peirce, *CP* 5.402.

3. Christopher Hookway, *Truth, Rationality, and Pragmatism: Themes from Peirce* (Oxford: Oxford University Press, 2000), 21–43.

4. Peirce, *EP* 1: 139, with my substitutions of "inquirers."

5. Compare with these expositions: Cheryl J. Misak, *Truth and the End of Inquiry: A Peircean Account of Truth* (Oxford: Oxford University Press, 1991); Elizabeth F. Cooke, *Peirce's Pragmatic Theory of Inquiry: Fallibilism and*

Indeterminacy (London and New York: Continuum, 2007); Christopher Hookway, *The Pragmatic Maxim: Essays on Peirce and Pragmatism* (Oxford: Oxford University Press, 2012).

6. Dewey, *MW* 6: 37, 38.

7. Dewey, *MW* 6: 38–39.

Chapter 9

1. Terrence Deacon, *Incomplete Nature: How Mind Emerged from Matter* (New York: W. W. Norton, 2011); David Haig and Daniel Dennett, "Haig's 'Strange Inversion of Reasoning' (Dennett) and Making Sense: Information Interpreted as Meaning (Haig)" (2017), accessed August 2021 at http://philsci-archive.pitt.edu/13287/; Jeremy Sherman, *Neither Ghost Nor Machine: The Emergence and Nature of Selves* (New York: Columbia University Press, 2017); Alan Jasanoff, *The Biological Mind: How Brain, Body, and Environment Collaborate to Make Us Who We Are* (New York: Basic Books, 2018).

2. Dewey, *LW* 13: 324.

3. Scientific cosmology after relativity concurs. See Roberto Mangabeira Unger and Lee Smolin, *The Singular Universe and the Reality of Time: A Proposal in Natural Philosophy* (Cambridge, UK: Cambridge University Press, 2014).

4. Peirce, *CP* 6.268.

5. Dewey *LW* 1: 200–201.

6. Vagueness is inherent to all concepts, and not just meanings in symbols or terms in language. Consult theories of vagueness in Claudine Tiercelin, *Pragmatism and Vagueness: The Venetian Lectures* (Milan: Mimesis International, 2019); and Kit Fine, *Vagueness: A Global Approach* (Oxford: Oxford University Press, 2020). Fixity to a word's meaning is not due to rigid concepts intended by speakers, but to an illusion generated by a language's habitual utility. See Jody Azzouni, *Semantic Perception: How the Illusion of a Common Language Arises and Persists* (Oxford: Oxford University Press, 2013). On the myths of qualia and consciousness, see Daniel C. Dennett, *Sweet Dreams: Philosophical Obstacles to a Science of Consciousness* (Cambridge, MA: MIT Press, 2005).

7. James's radical empiricism as a method has been paired with neutral monism as a metaphysics. Erik C. Banks, *The Realistic Empiricism of Mach, James, and Russell: Neutral Monism Reconceived* (Cambridge, UK: Cambridge University Press, 2014). Eric James, *Routledge Philosophy Guidebook to William James on Psychology and Metaphysics* (London and New York: Routledge, 2009). David C. Lamberth, *William James and the Metaphysics of Experience* (Cambridge, UK: Cambridge University Press, 1999).

8. James, "Does Consciousness Exist?" *Works: Essays in Radical Empiricism*, 3–4, 13, 14.

9. James, unlike Edmund Husserl, does not subtract the observable world from ordinary experience to find a metaphysically primordial "subjectivity" with an indubitable essence of its own. For radical empiricism, after objectivity and subjectivity are treated equally as emergent, what is phenomenal is simply the world again. Dewey's treatment of "immediate experience" is the same maneuver. On pragmatism and phenomenology, consult Maria Baghramian and Sarin Marchetti, eds., *Pragmatism and the European Traditions: Encounters with Analytic Philosophy and Phenomenology before the Great Divide* (London: Routledge, 2017); and Jakub Čapek and Ondřej Švec, eds., *Pragmatic Perspectives in Phenomenology* (New York and London: Routledge, 2017).

10. Dewey, *Art as Experience*, *LW* 10: 268.

11. Dewey, *Art as Experience*, *LW* 10: 13.

12. A sampling of books must serve. Peter Godfrey-Smith, *Complexity and the Function of Mind in Nature* (Cambridge, UK: Cambridge University Press, 1998); Susan Hurley, *Consciousness in Action* (Cambridge, MA: Harvard University Press, 1998); Alva Noë, *Action in Perception* (Cambridge, MA: MIT Press, 2004); Richard Menary, ed., *The Extended Mind* (Cambridge, MA: MIT Press, 2010); Andreas K. Engel, Karl J. Friston, and Danica Kragic, eds., *The Pragmatic Turn: Toward Action-Oriented Views in Cognitive Science* (Cambridge, MA: MIT Press, 2016).

13. Peirce, *CP* 5.313. See Richard K. Atkins, *Charles S. Peirce's Phenomenology: Analysis and Consciousness* (Oxford: Oxford University Press, 2018).

14. Peirce, *CP* 5.212.

15. Scott Sehon, *Teleological Realism: Mind, Agency, and Explanation* (Cambridge, MA: MIT Press, 2005); Roman Madzia and Matthias Jung, eds., *Pragmatism and Embodied Cognitive Science* (Berlin: De Gruyter, 2016); Mark Johnson, *Embodied Mind, Meaning, and Reason: How Our Bodies Give Rise to Understanding* (Chicago: University of Chicago Press, 2017); Pentti Määttänen, *Mind in Action: Experience and Embodied Cognition in Pragmatism* (Cham, Switzerland: Springer, 2018); Jay Schulkin and Matthew Crippen, *Mind Ecologies: Body, Brain, and World* (New York: Columbia University Press, 2020).

16. This sort of example is discussed in James, *The Principles of Psychology* (New York: Henry Holt, 1890), vol. 1, 24–26; and Dewey, "The Reflex Arc Concept in Psychology" (1896), *ED* 2: 3–10.

17. Hilary Putnam, *Mind, Languages and Reality, Philosophical Papers*, vol. 2 (Cambridge, UK: Cambridge University Press, 1975), 227.

18. Dewey, *LW* 1: 179.

Chapter 10

1. Animals passing the "mirror test" for a sense of individuality are, not coincidentally, most of the species that display mourning behaviors over the death of a familiar conspecific: humans, chimpanzees, bonobos, orangutans, gorillas, bottlenose dolphins, killer whales, elephants, and corvids (magpies, crows, ravens). On animal mentality, consult Kristin Andrews and Jacob Beck, eds., *The Routledge Handbook of Philosophy of Animal Minds* (Abingdon, UK, and New York: Routledge, 2018).

2. Russell, *Logic and Knowledge*, ed. R. C. Marsh (London: George Allen and Unwin, 1956), 42.

3. Daniel Dennett, *Consciousness Explained* (Boston: Little, Brown, 1991).

4. B. F. Skinner, *The Behavior of Organisms: An Experimental Analysis* (Englewood Cliffs, NJ: Prentice-Hall, 1938); B. F. Skinner, *Science and Human Behavior* (New York: Macmillan, 1953).

5. Jean Piaget, *The Construction of Reality in the Child*, trans. Margaret Cook (New York: Basic Books, 1954); L. S. Vygotsky, *Mind in Society: The Development of Higher Psychological Processes* (Cambridge, MA: Harvard University Press, 1978).

6. George H. Mead, *Mind, Self, and Society from the Standpoint of a Social Behaviorist*, ed. Charles W. Morris (Chicago: University of Chicago Press, 1934), 140.

7. Dewey, *MW* 10: 63.

8. Noam Chomsky, *Language and Mind* (New York: Harcourt, Brace & World, 1968). Jerry A. Fodor, *Psychosemantics: The Problem of Meaning in the Philosophy of Mind* (Cambridge, MA: MIT Press, 1987). Pragmatism views pragmatics as the grounding stage, with semantics and syntax as developmental refinements. For an overview, see James Russell, *What is Language Development? Rationalist, Empiricist, and Pragmatist Approaches to the Acquisition of Syntax* (Oxford: Oxford University Press, 2004).

9. John R. Searle, *Intentionality: An Essay in the Philosophy of Mind* (Cambridge, UK: Cambridge University Press, 1983), 230; John R. Searle, *Making the Social World: The Structure of Human Civilization* (New York: Oxford University Press, 2010), 4.

10. Searle, *Making the Social World*, 44.

11. Susan T. Fiske, *Social Beings: A Core Motives Approach to Social Psychology* (Hoboken, NJ: Wiley, 2010), 128.

12. A sampling includes the following works: Michael Gazzaniga, *The Social Brain* (New York: Basic Books, 1985); Albert Bandura, *The Social Foundations of Thought and Action: A Social Cognitive Theory* (Englewood Cliffs, NJ: Prentice-Hall, 1986); James Wertsch, *Voices of the Mind: A Sociocultural Approach to*

Mediated Action (Cambridge, MA: Harvard University Press, 1991); Radu Bogdan, *Minding Minds: Evolving a Reflexive Mind by Interpreting Others* (Cambridge, MA: MIT Press, 2000); Philippe Rochat, *Others in Mind: Social Origins of Self-Consciousness* (Cambridge, UK: Cambridge University Press, 2009).

13. Albert Newen, Shaun Gallagher, and Leon De Bruin, eds., *The Oxford Handbook of 4E Cognition* (Oxford: Oxford University Press, 2018); Michael D. Kirchhoff and Julian Kiverstein, *Extended Consciousness and Predictive Processing: A Third-Wave View* (London and New York: Routledge, 2019); Kirk Ludwig and Marija Jankovic, eds., *The Routledge Handbook of Collective Intentionality* (Abingdon, UK and New York: Routledge, 2017).

14. Eliot R. Smith and Frederica Conrey, "The Social Context of Cognition," in *Cambridge Handbook of Situated Cognition*, eds. P. Robbins and M. Aydede (Cambridge, UK: Cambridge University Press, 2009), 456.

15. Robin Dunbar, Clive Gamble, and John Gowlett, eds., *Social Brain, Distributed Mind* (Oxford: Oxford University Press, 2010); Clive Gamble, John Gowlett, and Robin Dunbar, *Thinking Big: How the Evolution of Social Life Shaped the Human Mind* (London: Thames and Hudson, 2014).

16. Amy A. Weimer, Katherine Rice Warnell, Idean Ettekal, Kelly B. Cartwright, Nicole R. Guajardo, and Jeffrey Liew, "Correlates and Antecedents of Theory of Mind Development during Middle Childhood and Adolescence: An Integrated Model," *Developmental Review* 59 (March 2021): 100945; Lisa M. Oakes and David H. Rakison, *Developmental Cascades: Building the Infant Mind* (Oxford: Oxford University Press, 2019); Jean Decety, ed., *The Social Brain: A Developmental Perspective* (Cambridge, MA: MIT Press, 2020).

17. Anthony D. Pellegrini, *The Role of Play in Human Development* (Oxford: Oxford University Press, 2009).

18. Peirce, *CP* 5.421.

19. For twentieth century philosophers, the terms of debate over the combination of idealism, collectivism, and socialism were set by Bernard Bosanquet's defense in *The Philosophical Theory of the State* (London: George Allen and Unwin, 1899); and L. T. Hobhouse's response in *The Metaphysical Theory of the State: A Criticism* (London: George Allen and Unwin, 1918).

20. Michael E. Bratman, *Shared Agency: A Planning Theory of Acting Together* (Oxford: Oxford University Press, 2014); John Cacioppo, Penny Visser, and Cynthia Pickett, eds., *Social Neuroscience: People Thinking about Thinking People* (Cambridge, MA: MIT Press, 2006); David D. Franks, *Neurosociology* (New York: Springer, 2010); Christian List and Philip Pettit, *Group Agency: The Possibility, Design, and Status of Corporate Agents* (Oxford: Oxford University Press,

2011); Dermot Moran and Thomas Szanto, eds., *Phenomenology of Sociality: Discovering the "We"* (New York and London: Routledge, 2016).

21. While naturalistic, this *empowerment* view of freedom is not yet another compatibilism, or an agent–causal account. The determinism vs. indeterminism debate is irrelevant to intelligent practice. Insects do not freely will what they do, not because they don't determine their actions, but because they can't control their reactions. Dewey, *Human Nature and Conduct: An Introduction to Social Psychology* (New York: Henry Holt, 1922), 303–305; Daniel Dennett, *Freedom Evolves* (New York: Viking, 2003).

Chapter 11

1. Joseph Henrich, *The Secret of Our Success: How Culture is Driving Human Evolution* (Princeton, NJ: Princeton University Press, 2016), 35.

2. Michael Tomasello, *Becoming Human: A Theory of Ontogeny* (Cambridge, MA: Harvard University Press, 2019); John Parrington, *Mind Shift: How Culture Transformed the Human Brain* (Oxford: Oxford University Press, 2021); Laurence J. Kirmayer, Carol M. Worthman, Shinobu Kitayama, Robert Lemelson, and Constance Cummings, eds., *Culture, Mind, and Brain: Emerging Concepts, Models, and Applications* (Cambridge, UK: Cambridge University Press, 2020).

3. Melvin Konner, *The Evolution of Childhood: Relationships, Emotion, Mind* (Cambridge, MA: Harvard University Press, 2010); Michael Tomasello, *A Natural History of Human Thinking* (Cambridge, MA: Harvard University Press, 2014).

4. Michael C. Corballis. *The Recursive Mind: The Origins of Human Language, Thought, and Civilization* (Princeton, NJ: Princeton University Press, 2011). See also Ronald J. Planer and Kim Sterelny, *From Signal to Symbol: The Evolution of Language* (Cambridge, MA: MIT Press, 2021).

5. Robin Dunbar connects a scale of orders of intentionality to stages of pre-*sapiens* evolution in "The Social Brain and the Cultural Explosion of the Human Revolution," in *Rethinking the Human Revolution: New Behavioural and Biological Perspectives on the Origin and Dispersal of Modern Humans*, eds. Paul Mellars, Katie Boyle, Ofer Bar-Yosef, and Chris Stringer (Cambridge, UK: McDonald Institute, 2007), 91–98. See also Nathan Oesch and Robin Dunbar, "The Emergence of Recursion in Human Language: Mentalising Predicts Recursive Syntax Task Performance," *Journal of Neurolinguistics* 43 (August 2017): 95–106; John Gowlett, Clive Gamble, and Robin Dunbar, "Human Evolution and the Archaeology of the Social Brain," *Current Anthropology* 53.6 (December 2012): 693–710; Thomas Wynn and Frederick Coolidge, "Archeological

Insights into Hominin Cognitive Evolution," *Evolutionary Anthropology* 25.4 (2016): 200–213.

6. In the words of Robert Bierstedt, *American Sociological Theory: A Critical History* (New York: Academic Press, 1981), 98; Cooley's theory of the social self is in *Human Nature and the Social Order* (New York: Charles Scribner's Sons, 1902), chaps. 5–6; and *Social Organization: A Study of the Larger Mind* (New York: Charles Scribner's Sons, 1909).

7. Several key stages for cultural development could be discriminated. See Alan Barnard, "Unity versus Interdisciplinarity: A Future for Anthropology," *Current Anthropology* 57.3 (2016): S145–S153. Recent work on cognitive paleoanthropology and cultural evolution includes the following: Daniel H. Lende and Greg Downey, eds., *The Encultured Brain: An Introduction to Neuroanthropology* (Cambridge, MA: MIT Press, 2012); R. I. M. Dunbar, Clive Gamble, and J. A. J. Gowlett, eds., *Lucy to Language: The Benchmark Papers* (Oxford: Oxford University Press, 2014); Thomas Wynn and Frederick Coolidge, eds., *Cognitive Models in Palaeolithic Archaeology* (Oxford: Oxford University Press, 2016); Christoph Durt, Thomas Fuchs, and Christian Tewes, eds., *Embodiment, Enaction, and Culture: Investigating the Constitution of the Shared World* (Cambridge, MA: MIT Press, 2017); Karenleigh A. Overmann and Frederick L. Coolidge, eds., *Squeezing Minds From Stones: Cognitive Archaeology and the Evolution of the Human Mind* (Oxford: Oxford University Press, 2019); Anna Marie Prentiss, ed., *Handbook of Evolutionary Research in Archaeology* (Cham, Switzerland: Springer International, 2019); Tracy Henley, Matt Rossano, and Edward Kardas, eds., *Handbook of Cognitive Archaeology* (London and New York: Routledge, 2019).

8. Dewey, *LW* 6: 32.

9. Joseph Margolis, *Historied Thought, Constructed World* (Berkeley: University of California Press, 1995); Roberta Dreon, *Human Landscapes: Contributions to a Pragmatist Anthropology* (Albany: State University of New York Press, 2022).

10. Kim Sterelny, *The Evolved Apprentice: How Evolution Made Humans Unique* (Cambridge, MA: MIT Press, 2012); Kim Sterelny, *The Pleistocene Social Contract: Culture and Cooperation in Human Evolution* (Oxford: Oxford University Press, 2021).

11. False inner representations persisting from environmental conditions seem improbable or inexplicable on rationalist terms, but even misguided reperformatives still function for improvable behaviors. See M. H. Bickhard, "The Emergence of Persons," in *Embodiment, Enaction, and Culture*, eds. Christoph Durt, Thomas Fuchs, and Christian Tewes (Cambridge, MA: MIT Press, 2017), 201–213.

12. Abductive experimentalism adequately justifies scientific realism. See John R. Shook, "Abduction, Complex Inferences, and Emergent Heuristics of Scientific Inquiry" and "Abduction, the Logic of Scientific Creativity, and Scientific Realism" in *Abduction in Cognition and Action*, eds. John R. Shook and Sami Paavola (Cham, Switzerland, 2021), 177–206, 207–227.

13. Leo Townsend, Preston Stovall, and Hans Bernhard Schmid, eds., *The Social Institution of Discursive Norms* (Abingdon, UK and New York: Routledge, 2021); Joseph Margolis, *Selves and Other Texts: The Case for Cultural Realism* (University Park, PA: Penn State University Press, 2001).

FURTHER READING

Charles Sanders Peirce

Collected Papers of Charles S. Peirce. 8 vols. Edited by Charles Hartshorne and Paul Weiss (vols. 1–6) and Arthur Burks (vols. 7–8). Cambridge, MA: Harvard University Press, 1931–1958. Citations are given by *CP* with volume and paragraph numbers.

Writings of Charles S. Peirce. Peirce Edition Project. Bloomington: Indiana University Press, 1982–present.

Volume 1, 1857–1866. Max H. Fisch, General Editor. 1982.

Volume 2, 1867–1871. Edward C. Moore, General Editor. 1984.

Volume 3: 1872–1878. Max H. Fisch, Senior Editor. 1986.

Volume 4: 1879–1884. Max H. Fisch, Senior Editor. 1989.

Volume 5: 1884–1886. Max H. Fisch, Senior Editor. 1993.

Volume 6: 1887–1890. Nathan Houser, General Editor. 1999.

Volume 7: forthcoming.

Volume 8: 1890–1892. Nathan Houser, General Editor. 2009.

The Essential Peirce. Vol. 1, 1867–1893. Vol. 2, 1893–1913. Peirce Edition Project. Bloomington: Indiana University Press, 1991, 1998. Citations are given by *EP*, volume number, and page number.

Pragmatism as a Principle and Method of Right Thinking: The 1903 Harvard Lectures on Pragmatism. Edited by Patricia Ann Turrisi. Albany: State University of New York Press, 1997.

Illustrations of the Logic of Science. Edited by Cornelis de Waal. Chicago: Open Court, 2014.

William James

The Works of William James, 18 vols. Frederick Burkhardt, General Editor; Fredson Bowers, Textual Editor; Ignas K. Skrupskelis, Associate Editor. Cambridge, MA: Harvard University Press, 1975–1984.

Citations are given by *Works* followed by book title and page numbers.

The Meaning of Truth, 1975.

Pragmatism, 1975.

Essays in Radical Empiricism, 1976.

A Pluralistic Universe, 1977.

Essays in Philosophy, 1978.

Some Problems of Philosophy, 1979.

The Will to Believe and Other Essays, 1979.

The Principles of Psychology, 3 vols., 1981.

Essays in Religion and Morality, 1982.

Essays in Psychology, 1983.

Talks to Teachers on Psychology, 1983.

Psychology, Briefer Course, 1984.

The Varieties of Religious Experience, 1985.

Essays in Psychical Research, 1986.

Essays, Comments, and Reviews, 1987.

Manuscript Essays and Notes, 1988.

The Writings of William James. Edited with an introduction by John J. McDermott. Chicago: University of Chicago Press, 1978.

Writings 1878–1899 of William James. Edited by Gerald E. Meyers. New York: The Library of America, 1987.

Writings 1902–1910 of William James. Edited by Bruce Kuklick. New York: The Library of America, 1987.

The Essential William James. Edited by John R. Shook. Amherst, NY: Prometheus Books, 2011.

John Dewey

The Early Works of John Dewey, 1882–1898. 5 vols. Edited by Jo Ann Boydston. Carbondale: Southern Illinois University Press, 1969–1972. Citations are given by *EW*, volume number, and page number.

The Middle Works of John Dewey, 1899–1924. 15 vols. Edited by Jo Ann Boydston. Carbondale: Southern Illinois University Press, 1976–1983. Citations are given by *MW*, volume number, and page number.

The Later Works of John Dewey, 1925–1953. 17 vols. Edited by Jo Ann Boydston. Carbondale: Southern Illinois University Press, 1981–1990. Citations are given by *LW*, volume number, and page number.

The Philosophy of John Dewey. Edited by John J. McDermott. Chicago: University of Chicago Press, 1989.

The Essential Dewey, 2 volumes. Volume 1: *Pragmatism, Education, Democracy*. Volume 2, *Ethics, Logic, Psychology*. Edited by Larry A. Hickman and Thomas M. Alexander. Bloomington: Indiana University Press, 1998. Citations given by *ED* with volume number and page number.

George Herbert Mead

The Philosophy of the Present. Edited by Arthur E. Murphy. La Salle, IL: Open Court, 1932.

Mind, Self, and Society from the Standpoint of a Social Behaviorist. Edited by Charles W. Morris. Chicago: University of Chicago Press, 1934.

Movements of Thought in the Nineteenth Century. Edited by Merritt H. Moore. Chicago: University of Chicago Press, 1936.

The Philosophy of the Act. Edited by Charles W. Morris in collaboration with J. M. Brewster, A. M. Dunham, and D. L. Miller. Chicago: University of Chicago Press, 1938.

Selected Writings: George Herbert Mead. Edited by Andrew Reck. Chicago: University of Chicago Press, 1981.

George Herbert Mead on Social Psychology. Edited by Anselm L. Strauss. Chicago: University of Chicago Press, 1964.

Secondary Literature

Alexander, Thomas M. *The Human Eros: Eco-ontology and the Aesthetics of Existence*. New York: Fordham University Press, 2013.

Allen, Gay Wilson. *William James, a Biography*. New York: Viking Press, 1967.

Apel, Karl-Otto. *Charles S. Peirce: From Pragmatism to Pragmaticism*. Amherst: University of Massachusetts Press, 1981.

Atkin, Albert. *Peirce*. London: Routledge, 2016.

Bacon, Michael. *Pragmatism: An Introduction*. Cambridge, UK: Polity, 2012.

Bernstein, Richard J. *The Pragmatic Turn*. Cambridge, UK: Polity, 2010.

Bird, Graham. *William James*. London and New York: Routledge and Kegan Paul, 1986.

Bjork, Daniel W. *William James: The Center of His Vision*. New York: Columbia University Press, 1988.

Blumer, Herbert. *George Herbert Mead and Human Conduct*, ed. Thomas J. Morrione. Walnut Creek, CA: AltaMira Press, 2004.

Bordogna, Francesca. *William James at the Boundaries: Philosophy, Science, and the Geography of Knowledge*. Chicago: University of Chicago Press, 2008.

Burke, F. Thomas. *What Pragmatism Was*. Bloomington: Indiana University Press, 2013.

Calcattera, Rosa Maria. *Contingency and Normativity: In Dialogue with Richard Rorty*. Leiden, Netherlands: Brill, 2019.

Carreira da Silva, Filipe. *G. H. Mead: A Critical Introduction*. Cambridge, UK: Polity, 2007.

Cochran, Molly, ed. *The Cambridge Companion to Dewey*. Cambridge, UK: Cambridge University Press, 2010.

Colapietro, Vincent M. *Peirce's Approach to the Self: A Semiotic Perspective on Human Subjectivity*. Albany: State University of New York Press, 1989.

Cooke, Elizabeth F. *Peirce's Pragmatic Theory of Inquiry: Fallibilism and Indeterminacy*. London and New York: Continuum, 2007.

Deledalle, Gérard. *Charles S. Peirce's Philosophy of Signs*. Bloomington: Indiana University Press, 2000.

de Waal, Cornelis. *Introducing Pragmatism: A Tool for Rethinking Philosophy*. Abingdon, UK: Routledge, 2021.

Fesmire, Steven. *Dewey*. London and New York: Routledge, 2015.

Fesmire, Steven, ed. *The Oxford Handbook of Dewey*. Oxford: Oxford University Press, 2019.

Gava, Gabriele. *Peirce's Account of Purposefulness: A Kantian Perspective*. London and New York: Routledge, 2014.

Goodman, Russell B. *Wittgenstein and William James*. Cambridge: Cambridge University Press, 2002.

Hickman, Larry A. *Pragmatism as Post-postmodernism: Lessons from John Dewey*. New York: Fordham University Press, 2007.

Hull, Kathleen A., and Richard K. Atkins, ed. *Peirce on Perception and Reasoning: From Icons to Logic*. London and New York: Routledge, 2017.

Joas, Hans, and Daniel R. Huebner, eds. *The Timeliness of George Herbert Mead*. Chicago: University of Chicago Press, 2016.

Kitcher, Philip. *Preludes to Pragmatism: Toward a Reconstruction of Philosophy*. Oxford: Oxford University Press, 2012.

Klein, Alexander, ed. *The Oxford Handbook of William James*. Oxford: Oxford University Press, 2022.

Maddalena, Giovanni. *The Philosophy of Gesture: Completing Pragmatists' Incomplete Revolution*. Montreal: McGill–Queen's University Press, 2015.

Malachowski, Alan, ed. *The Cambridge Companion to Pragmatism*. Cambridge, UK: Cambridge University Press, 2013.

Malachowski, Alan, ed. *A Companion To Rorty*. Malden, MA: Wiley-Blackwell, 2020.

Margolis, Joseph. *The Critical Margolis*, ed. Russell Pryba. Albany: State University of New York Press, 2021.

Martin, Jay. *The Education of John Dewey: A Biography*. New York: Columbia University Press, 2003.

Mayorga, Rosa. *From Realism to "Realicism": The Metaphysics of Charles Sanders Peirce*. Lanham, MD: Lexington Books, 2007.

McGranahan, Lucas. *Darwinism and Pragmatism: William James on Evolution and Self-Transformation*. London and New York: Routledge, 2017.

Merrell, Floyd. *Peirce, Signs and Meaning*. Toronto: University of Toronto Press, 1997.

Misak, Cheryl, ed. *The Cambridge Companion to Peirce*. Cambridge, UK: Cambridge University Press, 2004.

Parker, Kelly A. *The Continuity of Peirce's Thought*. Nashville: Vanderbilt University Press, 1998.

Price, Huw. *Naturalism Without Mirrors*. Oxford: Oxford University Press, 2011.

Rescher, Nicholas. *Pragmatism: The Restoration of its Scientific Roots*. New Brunswick, NJ: Transaction Publishers, 2012.

Richardson, Joan. *Pragmatism and American Experience: An Introduction*. Cambridge, UK: Cambridge University Press, 2014.

Rosenthal, Sandra B. *Charles Peirce's Pragmatic Pluralism*. Albany: State University of New York Press, 1994.

Schneider, Herbert W. *A History of American Philosophy*, 2nd ed. New York: Columbia University Press, 1963.

Schulkin, Jay. *Naturalism and Pragmatism*. New York: Palgrave Macmillan, 2012.

Schwartz, Robert. *Rethinking Pragmatism: From William James to Contemporary Philosophy*. Malden, MA: Wiley-Blackwell, 2012.

Shook, John R. *Dewey's Empirical Theory of Knowledge and Reality*. Nashville: Vanderbilt University Press, 1998.

Shook, John R., and Joseph Margolis, ed. *A Companion to Pragmatism*. Malden, MA: Blackwell, 2006.

Spencer, Albert R. *American Pragmatism*. Cambridge, UK: Polity, 2020.

Thayer, H. Standish. *Meaning and Action: A Critical History of Pragmatism*, 2nd ed. Indianapolis: Hackett, 1981.

Whitehead, Deborah. *William James, Pragmatism, and American Culture*. Bloomington: Indiana University Press, 2015.

INDEX

JOHN R. SHOOK, PHD, is Associate Professor of Philosophy at Bowie State University in Maryland. He writes about American philosophy, science, ethics, and neurophilosophy. He is the author of *Dewey's Empirical Theory of Knowledge and Reality* and *Dewey's Social Philosophy*, coauthor of *John Dewey's Philosophy of Spirit*, and coeditor of *The Blackwell Companion to Pragmatism* and *Neuroscience, Neurophilosophy, and Pragmatism*.